KURT BROUWER'S GUIDE TO MUTUAL FUNDS:
How to Invest with the Pros

Kurt Brouwer

John Wiley & Sons
New York • Chichester • Brisbane • Toronto • Singapore

In memory of
my dad, Gene Brouwer

Library of Congress Cataloging-in-Publication Data

Brouwer, Kurt.
   [Guide to mutual funds]
   Kurt Brouwer's guide to mutual funds: how to invest with the pros/Kurt Brouwer.
      p. cm.
   Includes bibliographical references.
   ISBN 0-471-52128-0
   1. Mutual funds.   I. Title   II. Title: Guide to mutual funds.
   HG4530.B75 1990   90-34328
   332.63' 27—dc20   CIP

Printed in the United States of America
    10 9 8 7

Contents

Acknowledgments

First, I wish to thank the brainy folks at IBM for taming the computer and squishing its power into the box that sits on my desk. Without it, this book would never have been written. I now have a deep respect for any writer who wrote anything in the dark years B.C. (before computers).

I'd like to thank my editors, Katherine Schowalter and Steve Ross. Three journalists also went out of their way to help me tighten and focus the 450-page original manuscript. My deepest appreciation to Allan Sloan, senior editor at *Newsday*; Carla Fried, reporter at *Money*; and Chris Barnett, the feisty and prolific financial writer. Each of them made many helpful suggestions and spent precious personal time helping me.

Also, I'd like to thank Charles Schwab, Peter Lynch, Frank Cappiello, Michael Price, Stephen Lieber, Claude Rosenberg, Jr., Roy Neuberger, Mario Gabelli, and Jack Leylegian for being so generous with their time and intelligence. Though they all have very busy schedules, each went out of his way to block out time for me. Thanks again.

For background on the mutual fund industry, I am indebted to Cary Klafter, a partner with Morrison & Foerster, the San Francisco-based law firm. Cary is a specialist in investment management law and, in addition to our firm, he represents many mutual fund and investment management firms. My thanks also to John Foppiano and Robert Sherwood at Price Waterhouse for their help with Chapter 7.

I would like to thank my partner Steve Janachowski for his help with portions of the books and his steady encouragement and support. Though my nerves steadily frayed, he and our staff—Susan Crutcher, Betty Nakamoto, Bryan Olson and Randy Eyler — helped keep me on an even keel. Thanks again.

Finally, for my neglected friends and family, I really was busy and haven't forgotten you.

Introduction

STOP. BEFORE YOU TURN THE PAGE, THIS IS THE ONE INTRODUCTION YOU CAN'T AFFORD TO SKIP OVER.

I wrote *Kurt Brouwer's Guide to Mutual Funds: How to Invest with the Pros* to help you weave your way through today's investment minefield. Sure, you can learn by experience, but why take the risk of being blown up?

We live and invest in a world of extremes. Investments soar to the stratosphere and then plunge to dark depths. In the end, many investors find they didn't make any progress or any money even though they had a wild ride. But some investors sidestep the madness, keep cool, and avoid the highs and lows. They steer clear of the fracas at peaks and valleys, but make solid returns the rest of the time.

Chapters 1 and 2 introduce you to principles that will help you learn how to set your investment objectives and to pick and choose investments that make sense for you. Chapters 3 through 7 give you the techniques, the rules of thumb, and the red flags and green lights to get aboard commission-free, no-load mutual funds, the ideal investment vehicle.

You'll also sit down with some of the country's top investment pros: Charles Schwab, Peter Lynch, Frank Cappiello, Michael Price, Claude Rosenberg, Jr., Stephen Lieber, Jack Leylegian, Mario Gabelli, and Roy Neuberger. You may recognize some of these names, but several will be new to you. Most of them stay out of the limelight. Eight of the pros in this lineup represent investment firms managing over $50 billion for more than two million investors. Also, Charles Schwab & Co., Inc. has over 1.3 million active discount brokerage customers around the world.

If you want to find out how the smart money pros think, you're in the right place, reading the right book. You will meet Charles Schwab after reading Chapter 5 and Peter Lynch after Chapter 6. Chapter 10 is devoted to interviews with the other pros listed above, seven of the nation's top mutual fund portfolio managers and investment advisers.

You'll find out how these pros identify and develop simple, logical investment concepts. That's the easy part. What sets them apart is the hard work, discipline and emotional detachment they have perfected to avoid getting caught in the reigning investment fads and fancies.

Chapter 8 is called "Take the Time to Learn or It May Cost You Money—Lots and Lots of Money." It details the difficulties many investors encounter working through most brokerage firms. Chapter 9 focuses on retirement plans—painless, tax-deferred vehicles to increase your wealth. You'll learn about the different types available to you and how, as well as why, you should use them. In Chapter 11 we review bedrock investment concepts you need to get started investing with the pros.

There will be times when it seems as though I'm being repetitious. I am. **Certain concepts and concerns are so important they can't be stressed enough.** When you see a point being made more than once, pay attention. It's crucial and I want to drive it home.

On every page you will be able to rifle in on techniques to make or save you money. The goal is to help you profit from these strategies as you build your wealth and financial security. But reaching this goal does not require a full-time committment nor does it mean you have to be an expert on all aspects of mutual funds. This book is *not* an encyclopedia of mutual fund information. It *is* a method of using funds to help you reach a goal—financial independence. If you work hard and carefully follow the techniques in the chapters that follow, I know you will be successful.

If you make the commitment to work hard at learning this information, I will do what I can to help you personally. After you've finished the book and done your research, if you are still unclear on some concepts, you may write me for clarification.

Kurt Brouwer
Brouwer & Janachowski, Inc.
230 California Street, Suite 420
San Francisco, CA 94111

If you write, enclose a stamped, self-addressed envelope and be patient. I will respond, but it will take a month or two.

Now let's get started.

1

You Too Can Invest
With the Pros

Over the last 10 years, I've spoken to thousands of investors. And heard tales of misery from many, if not most.

Some lost money because they were gullible, others due to their greed. Many missed out on opportunities for low-risk profits because they were paralyzed—scared witless of any move into the stock market. Still others moved around often yet never seemed to make any money and get ahead. And a few were perennial cynics, quick to find fault but never having a solution.

But I've also met winners—Main Street investors who think and invest like Wall Street pros. Who plan ahead. Who have a goal and take the steps necessary to reach for their dreams. Who blend realism with intelligence and control their greed and emotions. People who make their money work as hard for them as they worked to earn it.

In the chapters to come, I'm going to go all out to turn you into a winner, too.

Here's the challenge: If you commit your time and effort to the step-by-step process we're starting, you will know more about mutual funds than 90 percent of the stockbrokers and financial planners in the country. Guaranteed. I'll supply the tools and techniques; you supply the time and effort. What do you say?

After my first edition came out, I received a letter from Richard J. Nickoloff in Thousand Oaks, California. In it, he said, "I have done the homework. As a result, I have sold some mutual funds and invested in others. And, you were right: I am better informed about mutual funds and their performance than is the financial planner I hired to assist me in choosing mutual fund investments. He admitted that to me at the last meeting. OK, I'm ready for Book II." Starting now, don't just read passively. Imagine yourself taking the steps I outline. To invest with the pros, you need to start thinking like one.

Don't worry that you might not be able to develop a solid portfolio of outstanding mutual funds. You will do it. You'll become a successful mutual fund investor if you are willing to concentrate on your goals and devote your time.

I'm going to show you how, by investing with the pros, you can do what the smart money does—buy when others are dying to sell, and sell when they are eagerly clamoring to buy. As a smart long-term investor, you need to learn how to take advantage of these crises. Handled coolly, calmly, and correctly, a crisis becomes your opportunity.

If you've already had a few investment nightmares, you've probably developed a protective coating of skepticism. You don't trust salespeople. You demand facts, not biased opinions. You know what not to do, but you still need information you can use to improve your life and your family's future. And if you're honest with yourself, you'll recognize that your investment program has room for improvement.

BEWARE: MISTAKES OF THE PAST CAN EASILY BE REPEATED

Over the past 17 years, I've seen three serious declines in the U.S. stock market. Each time, investors made the same mistakes—overenthusiasm in a rising market and then panic and desperation. Though we all feel strong emotions at market peaks and valleys, you can learn how to avoid the impulse to self-destruct. Over my years in the investment business, I have analyzed hundreds of my clients' portfolios, ranging from a few thousand dollars to many millions. Yet I never fail to marvel at how many people make the same basic mistakes. And I also can't help remembering the times I made similar mistakes.

A physician who was a client of mine had a sizeable portfolio that he counted on for retirement. An old family friend of his ran Advanced Micro Devices, the large semiconductor firm traded on the New York Stock Exchange. My client had purchased several thousand shares of the company's stock over the years. Even though the stock's price bounced around a lot, he had done very well with it.

The stock hit a high point of 41⅛ a share and then dropped down two points to 39¼ shortly before he was scheduled to retire. I suggested taking some profits and diversifying, since most of his portfolio was in that one stock. He reluctantly agreed, but said, "Let's wait till it hits 40 again." I thought it was silly to arbitrarily pick 40, and I again suggested selling immediately. But I was not insistent enough. I should have pounded on the desk and demanded to know, "Why risk retirement for 75 cents a share?"

I didn't insist. And he did. Risk his retirement, that is. Advanced Micro Devices immediately started to plummet and he held on all the way down. "I'll sell when it gets back to 35," he said, and then it was 30 and then 25. Now, years later (the stock is at $9), he's still praying for a turnaround.

I don't make that mistake anymore, and neither do the other investment pros you're going to meet. But this experience was earned the hard way, and it was painful. I hope you can learn the easy way by profiting from the lessons I've learned.

One of the biggest mistakes investors make is trying to "time" the markets. Market timing is a seemingly logical endeavor, and many people develop complex systems that analyze trading patterns in the market to determine the direction or trend of future movements. And, truthfully, there are some recognizable patterns in market movements. Using hindsight, we can see exactly where a turnaround occurred. Looking back, we can pinpoint where a bull market began pawing the ground and snorting. The hard part is looking ahead.

DON'T BANK ON MARKET GURUS; RUN YOUR PORTFOLIO LIKE A BUSINESS

Even though it may be tempting to listen to the enchanting sales pitches of the market timers and gurus, don't do it. You'll be giving in to feelings of insecurity, not overcoming them. Gurus bank on the fact that many investors mistakenly think they can't do well on their own

As each market savant falls out of favor, another springs up. Given the pay and working conditions, it's not surprising. After all, the humble guru can earn millions dispensing advice for cash. The surprising thing is that investors charitably forget how badly they were burned by the last market guru and hurriedly sign up just in time to be there when the next one flames out.

Your investment portfolio is like a business. To be successful, you need a strategic plan and management team to carry it out. You also need clear goals and a meaningful benchmark for measuring results.

Just as you wouldn't try to build a business based on a faddish product, don't base your present and future net worth on investment fads, fancies, and phony prophets.

Whether you represent a corporate retirement plan with hundreds of participants or yourself as a private investor, you want your money invested prudently, profitably, and with reasonable safety.

Like most investors, you have questions about market risk and the safety and security of your money. You want solid performance and an investment strategy tailored to your needs. And you want to make sure you are getting good value for the fees you pay.

If this sounds like your situation, read on. But if you are

looking for aggressive market-timing strategies or risk-free, "no money down" schemes, stop right here. This book is not for you.

BARON ROTHSCHILD HAD THE ANSWER: BIG GAIN, SMALL PAIN

Though I don't try to outguess short-term movements in the market, I do believe you can roughly identify high and low points in market movements; more on that in Chapter 4. But I subscribe to Baron Rothschild's statement that he would let someone else have the top 20 percent gain as well as the bottom 20 percent. All he wanted was the 60 percent profit in the middle.

Just so you understand where I'm coming from, let me tell you what I do for a living. Along with my partner, Steve Janachowski, I run a firm in San Francisco with the rather unimaginative name of Brouwer & Janachowski, Inc. We are investment advisers, registered with the Securities and Exchange Commission. We oversee $175 million for corporate retirement plans, trusts, and individual investors. Our clients pay us an annual fee (starting at four figures and ranging up). As we work strictly on a fee basis, we have no axes to sharpen. We simply want superior performance for our clients.

In Chapter 8 you'll learn about some of my experiences before I became an investment adviser. From my own personal experience working at large brokerage firms, I learned what really goes on. If you are relying on a broker, financial planner, or anyone who is paid on commissions, you're getting advice from someone whose interests are often opposed to your own. You want solid, long-term investment performance, but your broker only gets paid when you buy or sell, and if you rely on biased advice, you may learn an expensive and unnecessary lesson.

I've also learned a few expensive lessons. For example, no single investment will work well through all market cycles, so I use a balanced investment approach. For our clients, we do exactly what I think you should do: coattail with investment pros using no-load mutual funds.

The following results for October 19, "Black Monday," reveal a little-known side to mutual funds. A conservatively managed portfolio of several hand-picked mutual funds can really put the brakes on a market slide.

Dow Industrials	−22.6%
Standard & Poor's 500	−20.5%
Brouwer & Janachowski, mutual fund accounts	−7.2%

This is an average of all of our client's accounts. Though we wish we weren't down at all, these results were for investors who wanted growth as well as preservation of capital and income. If you want growth, you have to accept some risks as well. The key to successful investing is to preserve capital when the markets drop and to do reasonably well when the markets are moving up. You need a "crash-proof" portfolio that will let you sleep well, and I'm going to show you how to set up your own portfolio of top-performing mutual funds.

In our work we have analyzed the individual investment results of over 2,000 mutual funds nationwide, and developed a computer-aided ranking system to spot the top performers and find out what made them successful. Obviously, I can't tell you every fact we've learned in scrutinizing mutual funds and the people running them. But I can and will distill the principles, the cardinal rules, the guidelines, and the red flags and green lights, and I can and will bring you along when I talk with other investment pros, who will share their personal strategies and experiences.

In short, I know the secrets that will help you invest the smart way, right alongside top investment pros. And you're going to know those secrets too. I will help you develop a practical, sensible, goal-oriented investment strategy—a professional strategy. I will show you how to do your own homework, do your own research, make your own decisions, and chart a safe course through the murky and dangerous waters of the investment business. Stay alert and stay close.

2

To Invest with the Pros, You Have to Think Like One

Planning your next investment move these days can be like driving in the fog. Even if you manage to get home, your nerves are shot. Was it worth the aggravation? Or you may feel you've been left behind—stuck in the slow lane as a red Ferrari screams by at 80. The stock market has taken off, but your stocks haven't. Or you hear about takeovers and leveraged buyouts where savvy investors made a killing—but when you finally act, it's on a stale "hot" tip and your fingers get singed.

Before you spend time learning *how* to invest, first decide if you should be investing at all. Before you put money in mutual funds or other investments, think hard about your finances. Do you have good health and life insurance? Have you salted away several months' living expenses in a money market fund or a bank account? Have you contributed to your individual retirement plan (IRA) or your company's retirement plan? Make sure you have taken care of these personal investments before you look further.

BROUWER'S BASICS FOR BULLETPROOF INVESTING

Pros invest using simple, common-sense rules. They're human, too, so they need a disciplined work and decision-making environment. Sounds complicated, right? Don't believe it. Just follow these four steps:

- ☐ Set clear objectives and guidelines.
- ☐ Use investments that mirror your objectives.
- ☐ Coattail with the pros.
- ☐ Track results, cut losses, and stick with winners.

Let's go over each in more detail.

Basic #1: Set Clear Objectives and Guidelines

Before you can decide on one or more specific investments, you should know which types make the most sense for you. Decide on your investment objectives and risk tolerance. Skipping this step is like buying a car simply because it got a top rating in *Motor Trend* or *Car & Driver*. Ask yourself, "Do I need a new car?" and "How am I going to use it: do I need economy or speed? How important is it to me that a car can go from 0 to 60 in 5.3 seconds?"

Focus on your objectives, and think about your life and financial situation. A 35-year-old foreman working in an auto plant probably has different objectives than a retired widow. Setting your investment objectives is simpler than you think. There are two main goals:

Growth: You would like to have more money than you currently have.

Income and preservation of capital: You are reasonably happy with what you have and would simply like to keep it and earn some income.

In reality, most investors fall somewhere between these two extremes. They would like growth with some current income or income with some growth potential. Ask yourself, "What would bother me more: to lose some money if the market nosedives and my investments drop with it, or to be chugging along in first gear when the market takes off into overdrive and leaves me behind?"

Once you set your objectives, don't waver. You must set realistic goals *and* stick to them. Are you investing for growth? If so, remember there will be some "white knuckle" times when the market spins out on a sharp curve. If you panic and hit the brakes, you may sell out just before a turnaround. Then you'll really kick yourself.

If you are investing for income and safety, don't be upset when your conservative investments lag a roaring bull market. The worst thing you can do is allow the stock market's siren song to seduce you into switching your strategy in midstream. Most likely you'll change just when the market has topped out and is poised for a pullback.

Basic #2: Use Investments That Mirror Your Objectives

To determine which investments make the most sense for you, let's go back and study investment results from 1972 to the present. The following chart shows what investors would have earned in each investment. As you can see, stocks outperformed the other categories. But during that period, there were a few ugly down markets when stocks took a brutal beating.

INVESTMENT GROWTH (1972–1989)

S & P 500 Stock Index	11.4%
U.S. Treasury Notes	9.3%
90-day U.S. Treasury Bills	7.9%
Consumer Price Index	6.6%

You may be wondering, "Why is he talking about stocks and bonds? I thought this was about mutual funds." Even though this is a book about mutual funds, it's important that you have a feeling for the types of investments mutual funds use. This will help you in later chapters, when we start looking at specific mutual funds.

To measure the growth of stocks, I used the Standard & Poor's 500 stock index; this is an index that measures the average performance of a broad-based list of 500 of the largest publicly held companies. For bonds, I used 10-year U.S. Treasury notes; these are direct obligations of the U.S. Treasury Department issued in maturities ranging from 1 to 10 years. Treasury notes are issued in $1,000 increments and pay a fixed rate of interest twice per year.

In case you're wondering, I'm not ignoring real estate, but unfortunately, there is no reliable index of real estate values. I can only guess that real estate probably kept pace with or beat stocks for this period.

You will see the term "cash equivalents" throughout the book. It refers to money invested on a very short-term basis, usually less than 90 days. This could be money you keep in a bank, in a money market fund, in a U.S. Treasury bill or in some other safe investment that can be turned into cash with little or no risk to principal.

U.S. Treasury bills can be purchased at banks or brokerage firms, or directly from the Federal Reserve. They are issued for short periods, usually 3, 6, or 12 months. Treasury bills are issued at a small discount to the printed face value and redeemed at full price, or par value. In the chart, I used U.S. Treasury bills with an average maturity of 90 days.

To measure inflation I used the Consumer Price Index, which is determined by the federal government. The government does this by purchasing a "basket" of basic goods on a regular basis and then gauging the difference in cost.

Each of the indexes measures the total return of the specific investments. The total return on an investment includes dividends or interest and capital gains or losses. It's important that you understand this term. Many people confuse it with yield. Yield refers to the interest or dividend the investor receives; a money market fund yields five percent when a $1,000 investment earns $50 in income per year.

The term *yield* only makes sense with risk-free investments like federally insured bank accounts or money market funds, which are nearly risk-free. Why? Because the principal or capital you invested doesn't fluctuate. But the price of a bond or bond fund moves up or down each time interest rates rise or fall. When rates go up, your bond or bond fund is worth less; as rates fall, your bond or fund is worth more.

This is a result of the fact that the yield on most bonds is fixed. For example, if you own a 20 or 30 year bond that pays a fixed yield of 8 percent annually, that means you are getting 80 dollars per one thousand dollars par or face value [par value or face value refers to the amount printed on the bond. Most bonds carry a one thousand dollar par value which is the amount that will be paid on maturity].

When interest rates rise, your bond becomes less attractive and the price drops because the yield is fixed at 8 percent. If new bonds of similar maturity and quality as yours come out yielding 10 percent, why would anyone buy your bond at full price when it yields only 8 percent? To induce someone to buy your bond you would have to drop the price or discount the bond to the point where it had a yield of approximately 10 percent. In this case, your bond would have to be discounted to less than $830 in order to have a competitive yield. But if interest rates drop, your bond paying 8 percent would appreciate in price because of the same principle. If new bonds are paying 6 percent, a bond paying 8 percent would generally sell for a price well above par value or one thousand dollars.

This sensitivity to interest rate movements is stronger with long-term bonds. Though the principal value of short-term bonds also fluctuates when rates go up or down, it is much more stable because investors know in a few years the bonds will be redeemed at par or face value.

I used 10-year bonds in the chart because midrange maturities [Treasury notes and bonds come in maturities ranging from 1 to 30 years] are the longest that make sense for most investors. The reason is risk. A long-term bond with 30 years before maturity is far more volatile and risky than a 10-year bond. Unless you watch interest rates closely and are very careful, don't buy long-term bonds or bond funds.

Many investors have been seduced by a "high-yielding" fund that pays out a nice steady income. But what they don't realize is that their principal can shrink insidiously due to rising interest rates. When you compare performance of different bond funds, analyze the total return, not the yield. Using total return performance statistics factors in the effect of interest rates to give a more complete view of performance than yield alone.

As stocks had the highest return, should you put all your money in stock-oriented mutual funds? Probably not, unless you have a strong tolerance for risk. If you favor preservation of capital and income from your investments, should you put all your money in Treasury bond funds or money market funds? Again, probably not. Look at the rate of inflation compared to the return on bonds. If you factor in taxes, you can see that bonds or cash equivalents did not grow compared to the rate of inflation.

We don't know what the rate of return from these investments will be in the future, but we can say, for example, that stock funds are likely to outperform bond funds over most periods in the future. But then again, bond funds and money market funds won't suffer as badly in down markets. So, unless you have nerves of steel and can hang in there during those long periods when the stock market looks bleak, it makes sense to balance your investments.

Basic #3: Coattail with the Pros

Fred and Bill are on their way to the golf course. Fred says, "We're gonna be celebrating tonight."

Bill asks, "Why is that?"

"Because we're gonna make a lot of money off these two suckers I met."

"Who are they?"

"Just two suckers. I beefed up our usual bet to $10 a hole plus $100, winner take all, and those guys went for it."

"But who are they?"

As they pass by the driving range, Fred points them out.

Bill screams, "But that's Jack Nicklaus and Lee Trevino, I'm not betting against them!"

Bill wouldn't risk a few hundred dollars playing against Jack Nicklaus and Lee Trevino, but, like many investors, he tries to compete against investment pros who are every bit as good in their field as Jack and Lee are on the golf course. And when Bill plays with investments, he does it with a lot more than a few hundred dollars.

Does he really stand much of a chance? It's true there are steps he could take to improve the odds, just as a golfer could go out and practice religiously before teeing it up with Jack Nicklaus. But Bill is not going to work at it full time, so he will miss opportunities and probably overlook important warning signals. What are his chances of actually beating the pros at their game, on their turf? Not good.

Instead of trying to beat the pros, as Bill dreams of doing, why not join them? Many of the smartest people in the investment business run mutual funds. Mutual funds are investment vehicles that offer access to the top investment brains in the country, low minimum investments, flexibility, diversification, and a low-cost fee structure.

Basic #4: Track Results, Cut Losses, and Stick with Winners

To find the top mutual funds and other investments, you have to be part private eye, part bloodhound. But after you've invested, you have to become a watchdog as well—vigilant in protecting your assets. Fortunately, this does not have to be a full-time job. In Chapter 7, I will show you a simple method to track your fund investments.

More people spend their time looking at the paper to see what their stocks or mutual funds did each and every day. But daily or even weekly price fluctuations usually mean little. In fact, looking at them often hurts investment results, because it gets investors worried or excited and often prompts more buying and selling.

Most homeowners who bought in the 1950s, 1960s, and 1970s now own homes worth more than they paid for them. In some parts of the country, people have seen the value of their homes go up many times more than their original investment. Yet those same people can't seem to make any money in the stock market. Why? It's so much easier to buy and sell stocks or mutual funds than real estate properties, and there is so much more information available, shouldn't it be easier to make money? Yes, it should, but there's one problem. Most people have no idea what the essential element of investment success is, so they blindly thrash around in the market, while naturally doing the right thing when they buy a home. What's the big difference? Compounding.

When you buy a home, you don't really think about it as an investment. You buy it for the long haul, and you don't worry about it. No one goes around daily or weekly checking the price of homes in the neighborhood. If values went up, you wouldn't say, "Maybe I should sell today." You don't listen to the six-o'clock news to see what the price of homes did today. People buy homes and hold onto them for 10 or 20 years, often more, so small annual increases in real estate values have a chance to build, to compound over a long period.

Use a similar approach when making other investments. Take your time to make sure what you're buying is the best you can find. But don't let your worries about trying to time your entry into the market keep you from making any decision at all. And once you're in an investment, it's fruitless, pointless, and ultimately frustrating to check prices every day. In Chapter 7, I'll show you a better way.

DON'T TRY TO SIP FROM A FIRE HOSE

Getting reliable investment information isn't easy. And once you get it, you still need a system for using that information to make and carry out decisions. In order to make good decisions you need solid, objective information, true enough; but it should also be hard, factual information that is tightly focused to your situation. Instead, you are deluged by claims and counterclaims, meaningless facts, biased opinions, and, here and there, a useful item or two. It's like a thirsty person trying to take a sip of water from a fire hose.

Remember that newspapers, television, radio, and most magazines have to come up with news every day. In writing about investments, they usually concentrate on short-term results. This fixation on what's happening *today* can distract you from the long-term outlook that is critical to investment success. Think of your investments as three- to five-year propositions, and structure them with a long-term view in mind.

The chief accomplishment of radio, television, and newspapers is the instantaneous transmission of information. Unfortunately, the ability to seek out important "news" has not kept pace with improvements in technology. Radio and TV, in particular, have a great talent for filling our heads with information that is superfluous to investing. These types of media are best suited to short, clear-cut pieces of information: "Stocks were up 31 points. Volume was 137 million shares. The day's top stocks were . . . ." These are factual bits of data that are easily gathered and reported, even though they mean almost nothing to a serious investor because they only focus in short-term gyrations not the broad, long-term trend.

Every night, all across the country, television's talking heads solemnly discuss today's market activity. "The market went down on rumors of the President's being ill." The next day, as you guessed, they will tell us the market went up because it turned out the President wasn't ill. Most short-term market activity is simply random, so don't drive yourself to the brink trying to make sense of it. And if you aren't going to act on information, why spend your time getting it?

STEP BACK AND YOU'LL SEE MORE

Still, many people think they'll miss something very important if they don't read and watch everything. On the contrary, it is only by stepping back a little that you can see the big picture. How can you evaluate what you see and hear? Just use common sense.

One quick example: If someone had a proven way to predict short-term swings in the stock market or in interest rates, do you think they would tell you about it? If you knew how to accurately predict the market, you could make millions or billions. Is it logical to think you would give up this immensely valuable information? No. I wouldn't give up the information if I had it, and neither would you. Common sense tells us this. Don't downgrade the value of your judgment, intuition, and common sense.

DARLING ONE YEAR, DOG THE NEXT

To be successful, you have to stick with winners. But over what time period do we measure? The best way to judge funds is over a full market cycle of five years or more, long enough to include both an "up" and a "down" market (see Chapter 5). The best-performing fund or investment in any one year is seldom the best over a long period of time. Why? Look at mutual funds that make it to the top of the list in any one year. They're generally specialized funds, such as international funds, single-industry or sector funds, gold funds, or aggressive growth funds (more on the different types of funds in Chapter 3). While these funds can have a year or two of extraordinarily high returns, they often follow that with a big loss.

Sector funds, or single-industry funds, were the best-performing group during the first nine months of 1987. Lipper Analytical Services reports the average sector fund was up 37.3 percent for that period. But then, in the month of October, the average sector fund plunged 34.1 percent, giving up over 91 percent of the year's gain. When you figure that most sector funds charge a small commission to buy in, you can see that full-year investors had a wild ride, but that's about it. Now think about those who got in late in the game. They would have suffered the 34.1 percent loss without having the big gain earlier in the year. It's better to stick with funds that have done well over a long period, funds that have proved their ability to deal with both "up" and "down" markets.

Remember the basics for protecting—and growing—your assets:

- [ ] Set clear objectives and guidelines.
- [ ] Use investments that mirror your objectives.
- [ ] Coattail with the pros.
- [ ] Track results, cut losses, and stick with winners.

Investing for your future requires planning and realistic self-appraisal. Decide where you want to go and how and when you want to get there. You need to select good investment vehicles and you need a good road map—but you still have to get in and turn the key. And, if you see that red Ferrari getting a speeding ticket—try not to gloat too much.

3

Mutual Funds: Terrific Tools for a Better Bottom Line

When he set out for America in 1870, 25-year-old Robert Fleming never dreamed his trip would change the way people invest all over the world. Fleming, a lowly bookkeeper in a textile mill in the prosperous Scottish town of Dundee, was dispatched to America to look after the investment interests of his boss, the mill owner. When he returned home, the now worldly-wise former bookkeeper told tales that excited his friends, who began to lust after a slice of the new world's abundant riches.

But neither Fleming nor his pals could cash in on the opportunity individually, so, in 1873, they formed the Scottish American Investment Trust. With a surprisingly small bankroll, they made history and got a sound return as well. Over the next six decades, Fleming had his hand in the formation of many investment trusts—the forebears of our mutual funds. Fleming's long, active, and highly successful career has made him the father of the industry, which now commands hundreds of billions in assets and millions of investors.

Recent statistics from the Investment Company Institute, a Washington, D.C.–based mutual fund trade group, show that there are 27 million individual investors in mutual funds plus an additional 3 million corporate, trust, and institutional fund investors. Millions have found mutual funds to be the easiest and best way to invest, and you will too. That is, unless you like spending your weekends poring over annual reports, proxy statements, prospectuses, charts, and graphs.

Fleming's instinctive conservatism led him to make sure the trusts he organized were diversified, carefully managed, and efficiently run. He also set the standard for investment management fees. Fleming's trusts had management fees of less than one-half percent of assets annually, and many mutual funds still hold to that standard today. For its time, the Scottish American Investment Trust was the perfect investment.

THE IDEAL INVESTMENT FOR EVERY MAN, WOMAN, AND CHILD

Mutual funds are the ideal investment vehicle because they offer professional management, low minimum investments, flexibility, diversification, and a low-cost fee structure. Full-time investment managers analyze investment opportunities for you. Mutual funds also offer a wide range of investment options and cerebral comfort, because they are more stringently regulated than most other investments you could consider. Leave it to a thrifty Scotsman to come up with the most cost-efficient and productive investment vehicle, the only investment that lets a small investor compete with corporate goliaths in the investment arena.

In the United States, the scandals that came out of the market crash of 1929 led to investment reforms in the 1930s, a historic period for legislation to protect the little guy. Of many pieces of legislation, the most important one for mutual fund investors was the Investment Company Act of 1940. This landmark law has made investment companies (legally, mutual funds are called investment companies) perhaps the most highly regulated investment vehicle.

The Investment Company Act of 1940 required mutual funds to have a very specific structure and operating style. Legally, a mutual fund is a corporate entity separate from its investment advisers—the people actually managing investments for the fund.   The fund has a board of directors, and there is a requirement for a certain percentage of outside, or independent, directors. Mutual funds are also required by law to provide shareholders and the Securities and Exchange Commission with detailed accounting and performance reports.

A QUICK LOOK AT TODAY'S MUTUAL FUNDS

(I Know This Won't Thrill You, But It May Enrich You)

The most common type of mutual fund is an open-end fund. The term open-end refers to the fact that this type of fund stands ready to buy back, at the net asset value (NAV), as many shares as investors want to sell. (The NAV is simply the net value of all investments held by the fund, divided by the number of shares outstanding.) In an open-end fund, the number of shares the fund has outstanding varies each day, because it depends on how many shares investors purchased or redeemed that day. Open-end funds can sell an unlimited number of additional shares based on investor demand.

Closed-end funds start out with a fixed number of shares. These shares are generally traded on a stock exchange or in the over-the-counter stock market, a computer-linked system of brokers who buy and sell stocks that do not have the size or financial strength to be listed on an exchange.

Unlike open-end funds, closed-end funds do not themselves redeem shares. Thus, shares change hands at whatever price buyers and sellers agree on. This price may represent a discount or a premium to the NAV of the shares, most typically a discount. There are several theories as to why closed-end funds generally sell at a discount to their NAV, but more important than that is whether the discount is widening or narrowing. Generally, discounts widen in bear markets as pessimistic investors dump shares; discounts usually narrow in a rising market.

To avoid paying taxes as a corporation, mutual funds must annually distribute virtually all of their net ordinary income and realized capital gains to shareholders. Many mutual fund owners forget about taxation (see Chapter 7). For now, suffice it to say that the dividends and capital gains distributions from a mutual fund are taxable (interest income from tax-exempt bond or tax-exempt money market funds excepted), whether the dividends are paid out in cash or reinvested in more shares of the fund.

HOW MUTUAL FUNDS ARE STRUCTURED

(Hang in There. You Need These Definitions and Insights)

Mutual funds have a specific structure, and as an investor, it's important for you to understand exactly how this works and how it differs from what you might do buying stocks or bonds or Treasury bills on your own. Let's examine the structure of a mutual fund. Once you understand how it works, you'll see the value of buying shares in a fund rather than trying to pick stocks or bonds on your own.

Every mutual fund is required by law to have the following structure:

Custodian to hold cash and securities: This is required under the Investment Company Act as a safeguard for the physical protection of your investment in the fund. Mutual funds must use a bank or some other secure institution to make sure your money goes where you intend it to.

Transfer agent: This may be the same institution as the custodian, or it may be another one. The function here is to administer the shareholders' account records as they purchase and sell shares.

Investment adviser: This is the fund's portfolio manager, who makes investment buy and sell decisions. This can be a single individual or a large firm. Many mutual fund investment advisers are subsidiaries of brokerage firms, who provide research, trading, and brokerage services as well as investment management.

Broker: The fund has to buy and sell investments and generally uses a number of brokerage firms. Some funds use one broker for most transactions, but most use many brokers. Because mutual funds have assets of millions or even billions of dollars, they get preferential treatment when they buy or sell stocks and other investments. If you were to walk in the door at a large full-commission brokerage firm and buy a few hundred shares of stock, you might pay forty or fifty cents per share for commissions. A mutual fund could buy those same shares for six or seven cents commission per share.

BILL, THE SAVVY GOLFER, GETS SLICED UP IN THE STOCK MARKET

Remember Bill, the golfer? He wouldn't bet against the pros on the golf course. Let's use him as an example to see what happens when an individual buys stocks directly through a broker. The scenario is this: Bill has $10,000 to invest, and he calls his broker, Samuel Bedford, for some advice. This is typical of what would happen if you placed an order at most large brokerage firms:

"Samuel Bedford."

"Hi, Sam, it's Bill, the golfer."

"Hello, Bill, what's up?"

"I have some money and I'm looking for a good investment. Do you have anything hot?"

"Well yes, we just had a new research report on Community Euthanasia. I just talked with the analyst and he thinks the P/E is low and the stock is undervalued. [*P/E* stands for price/earnings ratio. This number is calculated by dividing a stock's market price by its annual earnings per share.] When the earnings report comes out, the stock should really move. He said it could go from 9 to 15."

"Do you think it will? I mean, is the news about the earnings out on the street yet?"

"I doubt it; our analyst just met with the company yesterday morning."

"Well, I've got $10,000, do you think I should buy now or wait?"

"Well, it's offered at 9½, if it really moves, you'll be sorry you missed it."

"Okay, buy me 1,000 shares at the market."

Let's stop for a second and figure out what happened. Bill wants to hear a "hot" idea, something to get excited about. That's his first mistake. Good investing is not all that exciting—profitable and rewarding, yes, exciting, no. And remember, for better or worse, Bill's broker is really a salesman. The brokerage company expects Samuel to bring in at least $250,000 in commissions each year. So when a customer like Bill wants excitement, Samuel is probably going to help him find it.

Because there are several thousand brokers like Samuel in his firm, he probably didn't actually talk to the analyst. But he did listen to the analyst on the firm's morning call or "squawk-box" network during the morning sales meeting. (A "squawk-box" or "shoutdown" system is an internal communications system linking headquarters to each of the branches of a company. The firm has a daily schedule of market updates and research reports that brokers can listen to.) The analyst Samuel heard in the meeting gets much of his information directly from the company, so he knows as much or as little as every other analyst on Wall Street. While the analyst did meet with the company president, it was probably at a meeting attended by analysts from other firms as well. Even though some analysts produce useful reports, by the time this research report is written, printed, and distributed to thousands of brokers around the country, it's hardly a hot item.

Samuel hooked Bill with his own greed by developing a sense of urgency. "It's gonna move, and if you don't get in now, you'll be sorry."

So Bill went in and gambled $10,000 on a two-minute phone conversation. He's betting that his information and judgment about the stock being undervalued are accurate and that, miraculously, he's the only one who knows about this impending wonderful event—the release of a quarterly report on Community Euthanasia's earnings. Do you think this is a good bet?

Bill placed an order to buy 1,000 shares "at the market." This means that he's taking his chances on the floor of the New York Stock Exchange, because he will buy at whatever the price is when his order gets there. Currently, the stock is "offered" at $9\frac{1}{2}$ and "bid" at $9\frac{1}{4}$. The offer, or asking price, means someone is willing to sell at $9.50, and the bid price means someone will buy from you at $9.25.

To get back to the action, by the time Samuel writes the ticket up and walks it to the wireroom where it is transmitted to New York, the price has gone up to $9\frac{3}{4}$ offered. Remember, this firm has several hundred offices, so these things take a little time. Thus, Bill buys 1,000 shares at $9.75 each and pays a commission of $200, or roughly two percent of the total he put up. Total bill: $9,950.

You might be thinking the price could also have gone down. You're right, particularly if the whole market was dropping that day. But, in a case like this, it's likely the stock would move up a bit. Here's why. Bill's 1,000 share order comes in to Samuel's firm's post on the floor of the exchange, and they try to match it with any sell orders they've also received. They have no luck, because the research report was so good, many of the firm's several thousand brokers are putting in buy orders also. So the floor broker goes to the post where Community Euthanasia is trading, looks at the screen where the price is quoted, and sees an asking price of $9\frac{3}{4}$.

Who sets this price? Well, things get a little fuzzy here.

In the morning the specialist, an independent firm that is authorized by the exchange to handle that stock, arrives at a price by matching buy and sell orders and trying to get a feeling for the strength or weakness of the stock from the previous day's trading. The specialist is expected to buy or sell shares of the stock for his own account, in order to smooth out any mismatches in buy or sell orders. Because of all the buy orders from Samuel's firm, the specialist has to allow the price to go up in order to induce more owners of the stock to sell. He trades this stock every day and he follows all the news about the company, so he really is a specialist in Community Euthanasia. He's selling stock from his own account at 9¾ because he is confident this flurry of buying will probably die down and he can buy it back later in the day at 9¼. The specialist can profit from such a small move because he doesn't pay commissions.

Getting back to Bill, if he were to turn around and sell tomorrow, he would have to sell at the "bid" price, which is lower than the "asking" price (or what he paid). If the asking price stayed at $9.75, then the "bid" would probably be $9.50 per share for a pro commission total of $9,500. But, the way things often go is that the flurry of trading subsides and the stock goes back to $9.25 "bid" and $9.50 "ask." If Bill still wanted to sell, he would get $9.25 per share.

Samuel, the broker, takes another $200 for his efforts, so Bill nets $9,050 on the sale. His loss overall would be $900, almost 10 percent of his original investment. The example shows that whether Bill sells today or a year from now, the stock has to go up 9–10 percent just so he can break even

PURCHASE OF 1,000 SHARES OF COMMUNITY EUTHANASIA

Buy 1,000 Community Euthanasia at $9.75 =		$9,750.
	Commission	200.
	Total invested	$9,950.
Sell 1,000 Community Euthanasia at $9.25 =		$9,250.
	Commission	200.
	Total proceeds	$9,050.
	Net loss	$ 900.

after accounting for commissions and the effect of the spread between the bid and asking price.

How do mutual funds fit into this picture? Let's say the shares Bill bought were part of a large block of Community Euthanasia that was sold by a high-powered portfolio manager at a mutual fund. This professional has been following Community Euthanasia for 8 years. Even though the next earnings report is going to be positive, he worries about the long-term prospects due to changes in Medicare funding, which represents a large part of the firm's business. Since he follows the reports filed with the Securities and Exchange Commission, he also knows that several of the company's officers have been selling some of their shares. Officers of a corporation and large shareholders are required to file reports with the SEC when buying or selling stock in the company. Generally, it is considered a bad sign when a group of "insiders" such as corporate officers sell more of their firm's shares than they buy.

So the mutual fund manager decides to get out and take his profits. But when he sells, the cost structure is very different. Because he's selling a large block of stock, he gets preferential treatment. It's no different from the way an appliance store chain, buying in volume, can get a much better price than you could buying a stove at Sears. If you buy stocks or bonds on your own, you buy and sell at retail commissions. But a mutual fund pays a wholesale rate. As you can imagine, a mutual fund portfolio manager who has millions to invest (perhaps hundreds of millions, or even billions) is going to get very different treatment than our buddy Bill, the golfer.

Bill knows every rock, tree, and hazard on his golf course. Too bad he didn't know about the seven types of mutual funds before risking his money on Wall Street.

SEVEN BASIC TYPES OF MUTUAL FUNDS: FIND OUT WHICH ONES ARE RIGHT FOR YOU

The list on the following page shows the main types of funds along with the types of investment they generally use.

- Money market funds (Treasury bills, certificates of deposit, and commercial paper).
- Bond funds (corporate bonds, government bonds, and other high-yielding investments).
- Growth and income funds (stocks and bonds).
- Growth funds (stocks).
- Aggressive growth funds (stocks).
- Specialty funds (stocks in specific industries—oil and gas, gold, real estate).
- International funds (international stocks or bonds).

One widespread misconception about mutual funds is that they invest only in stocks. Not so. The two largest groups of mutual funds are bond funds and money market funds.

Money Market Funds: A Secure Garage for Parking Your Cash

The key difference between money market mutual funds and bond mutual funds is the average maturity of the investments they make. Money market funds invest in very short-term investments (under one year), and for this reason they have a very low risk to your principal. Money market funds usually offer check-writing privileges as well, to make it easier to take money out quickly.

Bond Funds: Plenty of Income and Safety, But Keep Your Eye on Those Interest Rates

Bond funds invest mainly in longer-term bonds (5 to 30 years). Recently, a number of short-term bond funds have come out. They generally use short-term bonds maturing in one to three years, and these have little risk to your hard-earned dollars. Intermediate bond funds buy portfolios of bonds with an average maturity of 10 years or less. Long-term bond funds generally use bonds with an average maturity of 10 years or more; these are the most volatile. For example, in April 1987, many long-term bond funds sank eight percent or more in value in a two-week period. The cause: a rapid jump in interest rates.

Growth and Income Funds: You *Can* Have It Both Ways

Mutual funds in the growth and income category (sometimes called balanced funds) typically commit from 50 to 90 percent of their assets to Fortune 500 stocks, such as Dow Chemical, IBM, and Pacific Telesis. The balance of the assets go into corporate and government bonds or cash equivalents.

Growth Funds: Highballing for Profits

Mutual funds in the growth category plunge more heavily into stocks—generally 90 to 95 percent of assets. But in addition to buying stocks of large companies, they also buy over-the-counter (OTC) stocks such as Apple Computer, Genentech and International King's Table. The smaller company stocks on the OTC market generally offer more growth potential, and more risk, than the more established companies on the New York Stock Exchange. This is primarily due to size. A small, growing company can double in size in a year, whereas large companies seldom grow that fast. However, large companies have better finances and more established businesses, therefore they are far less likely to fizzle and go out of business.

Aggressive Growth Funds: Really Putting the Pedal to the Metal

Funds in the aggressive growth category generally invest 90 to 95 percent of their assets in stocks; they typically put most of their emphasis on OTC stocks.

Specialty Funds: Putting All Your Eggs in One Basket Can Be Very Risky, or Very Rewarding

Specialty funds are also called sector funds. The most widely followed specialty funds have been gold funds, but there are many other types. In general, specialty funds concentrate their investments in one or two sectors of the market—energy, gold, health care companies, brokerage firms, or banks, for example.

Real estate funds are showing up as a new type of specialty fund. Rather than buying actual properties, they buy stocks of companies that own real estate. Though small now, this is a rapidly growing type of mutual fund.

International Funds: London, Tokyo, Australia, and West Germany Are at Your Fingertips

An international fund concentrates on foreign investments. It may be a growth and income, growth, aggressive growth, or even a bond fund. Some are conservative, some more aggressive. Most are broadly diversified, although a few concentrate all their investments in one country, such as Japan, Korea, Mexico, or Switzerland.

Many domestic funds also hold a significant proportion of foreign stocks in their portfolios—for example, Mutual Series, Fidelity Puritan, Dreyfus Fund, and Acorn Fund. Though each of these uses foreign investments, they have very different investment objectives and risk characteristics.

MUTUAL FUNDS USE THESE BASIC INVESTMENTS

Let's take a quick look at the basic investments that underlie most mutual fund portfolios. Funds place the bulk of their money into three major investment categories: stocks, bonds, and cash equivalents. To do a good job of selecting mutual funds, you need a basic working knowledge of the investments your funds will be making.

If you think we're going to run out and pick a top fund or two, you're wrong. The biggest mistake you could make now is to charge off with just enough information to be dangerous to your financial health and well-being. Aggressive, badly timed moves could lead you right into a stock market disaster. If you work your way through this chapter carefully, you will know more than most of your friends, relatives, or colleagues. So relax and keep reading. It's important.

Cash Equivalents: Instant Money

A cash equivalent is an I.O.U. with a maturity of less than one year. Money market funds are 100 percent invested in cash equivalents, but *all* other mutual funds use cash equivalents as well, to maintain a certain amount of liquidity, which facilitates shareholder redemptions and cushions swings in the stock and bond markets. Some examples of cash equivalents:

- □ U.S. Treasury bills.
- □ Certificates of deposit (under one year maturity).
- □ Commercial paper.

Certificates of deposit are issued by banks and savings and loan companies in various maturities. Amounts up to $100,000 are insured by agencies of the federal government. Commercial paper consists of short-term notes issued by corporations to raise money for normal operating purposes.

The two fundamentals of investing in cash equivalents are safety of principal and liquidity—the ability to pull your money out quickly. The yield or return is secondary to these concerns. Though you should always keep a modest reserve of five or ten percent of your assets in a money market fund or bank account, don't overdo it. Cash equivalents are not intended to be long-term investment vehicles; they are the parking places for money you may need soon. Investors got used to money market funds as a long-term investment when rates were high, but those days don't come around very often.

Veteran stock market investors like to keep money in cash equivalents or money market funds for the same reason gunfighters kept a few bullets in their belt—just in case. Money market funds are also a good place to keep "rainy day" money—three to six months of living expenses. They can also be used when you are saving for a down payment on a home or another big purchase.

Almost everyone needs a way to put money to work with minimal risk and maximum availability. But remember, you pay a high price for that liquidity, that immediate access.

The difference in return between a money market fund and a short-term bond fund can be a few percent each year, and over the years, that can really build up. Ask yourself if that immediacy is critical for all of the money you have in a bank account or money market fund. If not, consider the next type of asset—bonds or other types of fixed income. Fixed income simply means investments where you are essentially loaning your money in return for a fixed rate of return and a promise to repay the money at a specified date in the future.

Bonds or Fixed Income: When You Want a Stream of Cash

A fixed income investment is an I.O.U. with a maturity longer than one year. Fixed income denotes a broader category than just bonds. It includes bonds, mortgages, and other similar investments designed to provide income and relative safety of principal. But for simplicity, I use the term bonds or bond funds. Bond mutual funds, by definition, invest primarily in short, intermediate, or long-term bonds. Growth and income funds use bonds also. Examples of bond or fixed income investments:

- U.S. Treasury bonds and notes.
- U.S. Government agency bonds, such as Ginnie Maes.
- Municipal bonds.
- Mortgages.
- Certificates of deposit (long term).
- Corporate bonds.

Treasury bonds and notes are direct obligations of the U.S. Treasury, and both are issued in $1,000 increments. As we've seen, notes are issued in maturities from 1 to 10 years, and Treasury bonds come in 5- to 30-year maturities. Government agency bonds such as Ginnie Maes are obligations of the specific government agency that issues them. The term *Ginnie Mae* stands for the Government National Mortgage Association. This agency provides liquidity and stability to the home mortgage market by pooling individual home mortgages and selling them to the public.

Ginnie Maes are flawed investments. Because they are long-term bonds, if interest rates rise, they will suffer principal losses along with other bonds. But if rates drop, the underlying home mortgages are often refinanced. When the homeowner refinances, the investor receives his or her money back. Thus, the investor isn't able to lock in a high interest rate, which is the chief advantage of buying long-term bonds. Ginnie Maes are a case of heads you lose, tails you lose. If you can't win a coin toss, why take the risk?

Municipal bonds are issued by states, cities, and various state and local agencies. Money raised is used to build or maintain needed public facilities and services. Income from these bonds is generally free from federal income taxes and, usually, free from taxes in the state that issued them. Care must be taken to determine the security of principal and interest payments.

Corporate bonds are issued by companies and are less secure than government-backed bonds. As with municipal bonds, care must be taken to determine the security of principal and interest payments.

The world of bonds and other fixed income investments is incredibly complex, but there are some simple rules that govern it. For example, there is the yield curve. This term, though it sounds bizarre, covers a simple fact of life: Investors are generally willing to tie up their money for longer periods of time *only* if they get a *higher* rate of interest than they would for a short period.

Another basic rule is that interest rates are critically important in determining the value of a bond. When interest rates rise, the value of a bond drops, but when rates drop, the bond moves up. Over most longer periods, bonds have not been a wealth-building investment. And, in fact, they haven't done a particularly good job of preserving capital—after taxes and the ravages of inflation are taken into account.

The decade of the 1980s has been an extraordinary period for bond investors. The years 1980, 1981, and 1982 were brutal, as investors saw bond yields soar into the high teens, while the value of older bonds plummeted. But after that, interest rates began a steady decline, which produced extraordinary returns for bond holders. We've all heard about the great bull market in stocks, but few outside the investment business know that the total return (interest payments plus capital gains or losses) on long-term bonds outstripped the S & P 500 for several years from 1982 through 1986.

In Chapter 2 you saw that bonds were not spectacular investments over the 15-year period 1972–87. Let's go back further. For the period 1926–86, the return on 10-year Treasury notes was four percent. This is the total return, not just the yield. Since inflation (measured by the CPI) ran at three percent for that same period, you can see that a bond investor earning only four percent steadily lost ground to inflation if he had to pay income taxes on the four percent return. Over that same period, stocks returned a total of 10 percent, including dividends and capital appreciation.

Many investors pick bonds and bond funds by going for those with the highest yield. You should be more careful. Selecting bond funds by yield alone can be hazardous to your financial health and security, because the highest-yielding funds are usually the riskiest if interest rates move up sharply.

Stocks or Equities: Your Share of Corporate America

Stocks are a piece of the pie—ownership. Growth, growth and income, and aggressive growth funds invest in stocks, in varying amounts. Some examples of stocks, also called equities, are:

☐ Common stocks.
☐ Preferred stocks.
☐ Convertible preferred stocks.
☐ Convertible bonds.

Stocks represent a share of ownership in a corporation. Common stocks are generally the largest category of equity (net worth) a company has. Some stocks pay dividends and others do not, according to the profitability of the company.

Preferred stocks generally receive a fixed dividend. They are called preferred because they must receive their dividend before anything can be paid to common stockholders. They also usually have "preference" in a bankruptcy or corporate liquidation.

Convertible preferreds are preferred stocks that give the investor an additional right to convert them into common stock under certain conditions. Convertible bonds are corporate bonds that can also be converted into common stocks.

REAL ESTATE: WALL STREET MAY BE THE BEST PLACE TO BUY REAL ESTATE

Buying investment or income real estate poses special problems. Real estate usually involves a major financial commitment. For most people, making such a large investment results in extreme concentration of their assets. If you know real estate well and you are a risk-taker, that could be great. But for many people it's simply out of the question.

An alternative is investment in real estate investment trusts (REITs). These function much like closed-end funds (REITs are also traded on stock exchanges or in the OTC market). They have professional management and invest in a portfolio of real estate properties. But many have spotty records, particularly the mortgage REITs, which invested in mortgages secured by real estate, as opposed to the equity REITs, which bought actual properties. REITs first were popularized in the 1970s, just in time to crash in the commercial real estate bust of 1974–75. Since then the industry has improved to some extent, although recently several REITs ran into trouble in Texas real estate.

Some REITs have worked very well, primarily those that invested in income-producing properties, usually only modest amounts of borrowing, or leverage. REITs can be good investments provided they are managed well. The key, as in any company, lies with the people in management. They have to be working for the interests of the shareholders, not their own egos and corporate perks.

For those who don't want to pick and choose REITs and other real estate companies, a new vehicle is here—real estate mutual funds. Over the past two years several funds with a real estate investment focus have come out, and more are on the way. Funds of this type invest in REITs and other stocks such as those of real estate developers. Though the track records aren't long enough to analyze adequately, perhaps the small investor finally has a solid, well-diversified real estate investment—real estate mutual funds.

Two relatively new no-load real estate funds exist. These mutual funds invest in real estate investment trusts, common stocks of real estate developers, and other companies with large real estate holdings. Neither of these funds has a long performance record, but both have good management and solid investment strategies. They are:

☐ Evergreen Global Real Estate Equity Fund
☐ U.S. Real Estate Fund

Now that we've reviewed the basic building blocks that mutual funds use, let's go over more essentials of mutual fund investing. But before we do, take a breather. We've covered a lot of definitions and new terms. Though some of these terms may seem confusing now, you'll get the hang of them soon. That's a promise.

MUTUAL FUND FEE STRUCTURE: YOU PAY A LITTLE FOR A LOT OF EXPERTISE

All mutual funds deduct operating expenses, transaction costs, and management fees from assets in the fund. The easiest way to see what those are is to check out the expense ratio, a calculation of fund operating costs as a percentage of your investment. This amount is deducted from your account before anything is paid out or reinvested.

Typically, expenses reduce your return in a fund by from 0.7 percent to 1.5 percent, depending on the type of fund (stock funds usually have higher costs than bond funds).

Brokerage fees and certain other expenses are not included in the ratio.

Anything over 1.5 percent for an expense ratio is quite high, unless the fund is a small one, with assets under $30 million. The size of this fee is important because those costs come out of your return. For example, if a fund has a 10 percent return on investment with a 1.5 percent expense ratio, your net return would be approximately 8.5 percent. A lower expense ratio of 0.75 percent (that is, three-fourths of a percent) would boost your net return.

Information on a mutual fund's expense ratio can generally be found on page 2 of the prospectus in a table called "Table of Fund Expenses or Summary of Fund Expenses." (The prospectus is a basic document that mutual funds are required to send to investors before they buy in. It contains all the information the Securities and Exchange Commission thinks investors should know about a fund. See Chapter 5 for more details.) This particular section of the prospectus gives basic financial information on the fund. The specific line for the expense ratio is called "Total Fund Expenses or Total Operating Expenses."

"No-load" mutual funds are different from "load" mutual funds in that true no-loads do not impose a sales charge when you buy or sell. Load mutual funds levy a charge of up to 8½ percent of your investment, most of which goes to the broker making the sale. Some funds without a "front-end" load now charge a deferred contingent sales charge or redemption fee instead of an up-front commission.

Funds using a deferred contingent sales charge usually start at a four to five percent commission, but this fee is taken out only if you leave the fund. Typically, the rate to be charged declines one percent per year, so that if you stay in the fund for five years or more, you can then get out with no fee.

When you look at mutual fund quotations in the paper, you will see two headings for share prices. For example, the *Wall Street Journal* uses the headings *NAV* (net asset value) and *Offer Price*. Mutual funds with front-end loads or commissions, will have both values listed; they sell shares at the offer price, which includes the commission. No-load funds or funds with deferred contingent sales charges sell shares to investors at the day's NAV, and this is the only price listed for these funds.

12B-1—ANOTHER HAND IN YOUR WALLET

There's another, less obvious fee with the catchy name *12b-1*. This is an expense charged to a fund's assets each year. Funds can use these fees to pay for marketing and distribution expenses. A fund can use the 12b-1 provision even if it has other types of sales charges. Though 12b-1 payments are generally modest, you should check this out before you buy in (many funds have no 12b-1 fees, but others go as high as 1.25 percent). The information on this and other fees is in a table on the first few pages of the prospectus. Because figuring out all the fees is a bit time-consuming, the SEC now requires that a fee table be included on the first couple of pages of every prospectus to help you do a little price-comparison shopping.

The highest 12b-1 fee I have seen is that used by some of the Keystone mutual funds. They state in their prospectus that they may charge as much as 1.25 percent annually for 12b-1 expenses. If you plan to stick with a fund for several years, a one percent or higher annual 12b-1 bite out of fund assets can be the equivalent of a one-time $8\frac{1}{2}$ percent up-front sales charge. While the one-time front-end commission is higher initially, the 12b-1 charge hits you each year, so in the end it may be more. In spite of this, a mutual fund without a front-end load or redemption fee is allowed to bill itself as a "no-load" fund, even though it charges 12b-1 expenses. (I think the SEC should require funds that use a 12b-1 in excess of 0.25 percent to advertise as load funds.)

HELLO OUT THERE

Are you still with me? If you made it through this discussion of 12b-1 fees and other sleep-inducing topics, don't stop now.

We have one more short section on mutual fund families, and then you will have made it through a demanding chapter.

ALL IN THE FAMILY

Mutual funds, like children, seem to thrive in a family atmosphere. We seldom see a solo mutual fund anymore. The vast majority of funds are part of a larger family of funds, such as Fidelity, Vanguard, Dreyfus, Scudder, T. Rowe Price, Neuberger & Berman, Twentieth Century, Evergreen, and Janus Funds. This phenomenon is simply the result of economies of scale; mutual funds are "cheaper by the dozen." Mutual fund sponsors primarily make a living from management fees; therefore, they want to bring in more of your money and thus earn more fees. The prevailing wisdom for the "rocket scientists" of mutual fund marketing is to have a fund for everyone and every investment interest, no matter how specialized or bizarre.

There are some advantages for you in a family of funds, and most funds are delighted to extol the virtues of their telephone redemption privileges, exchange arrangements among mutual funds in the fund family, check-writing, or mind-boggling numbers of something-for-everyone sector funds.

Mutual fund marketing pros also know that with a broad range of funds, they stand a better chance of having a top-performing fund in one category or another. Thus, they can put out ads proclaiming themselves "number one" week after week. What they don't mention is that this year's top fund may have been a poor performer last year. These self-serving marketing techniques can, inadvertently, promote the "hot money" syndrome, in which investors are constantly switching from one fund to another looking for the next number-one fund. This doesn't work. Just when you thought you knew exactly which fund was the hot one, it changes. In Chapter 2 you saw that last year's top fund can be this year's dog. When an investor chases last year's fund, his or her money seems like the kiss of death—about the time it goes in, the fund turns cold. In Chapter 5 you will learn how to do your own research to find future winning mutual funds.

The biggest advantage in a family of funds—and this is generally found in smaller groups such as Mutual Series, Neuberger & Berman, the Evergreen Funds, Twentieth Century Funds, Janus Capital Corporation, and Pacific Investment Management—is that all of their portfolio managers share a common outlook or set of values. A fund in the group may have its own special investment objectives, such as growth and income or aggressive growth, but the same philosophy or set of values applies. Once you find a group of funds such as these, you can feel more comfortable with it than with a family that is simply held together by marketing skills.

Whether you buy into an individual fund or a family of funds, no-load mutual funds offer you more diversity and efficiency than any other investment form. They feature an enormous range of choices, and you can buy in with a modest outlay of cash. Minimum investment requirements run as low as $500 or $1,000, and subsequent investments are often much less. In addition, the professional, hands-on management of some of Wall Street's top brains is, by itself, an alluring attraction.

When you invest in funds, don't forget to say thanks to the first investment pro, Robert Fleming. And give yourself a mental pat on the back also. Winners are people who do what others are unwilling or unable to do. That means working at investment success while others simply talk about it. When you get the financial and psychic rewards of investment success, you will savor them that much more because you've earned them.

4

Set Your Sights
on Success

The market's a bullet train, but many investors are paralyzed—standing on the platform, wondering when to board. They may have the information, but not the confidence to move. And whether investors are already on board and in their seats or still waiting out in the cold, they know this: one wrong move and their nest egg, net worth, or retirement plans may get sidetracked. To avoid getting derailed, you should develop a balanced investment approach custom-made for you.

To begin, break things down into bite-sized chunks. As an investor you have a "want" list:

□ You have money to invest over and above what you need to live on. You want that money to work as hard for you as you worked to earn it.
□ You want the best return with the least risk.

□ You want a portfolio custom-tailored for your needs. You want to know and understand the alternatives that make sense for you, based on the amount you have to invest, the time you will spend, and the length of time you can afford to tie up your money.

□ You want a simple, effective way to measure risk and anticipate economic changes.

To go from wishes or wants to reality is possible, but it requires desire, drive, and determination. You have to pay your dues. Start by hammering out your personal objectives.

To win on Wall Street you must know yourself. How much risk are you willing to take? Are you conservative or aggressive? Take the time to get a clear picture of what you want.

Once you know your investment objectives, you still need a practical way to locate and buy mutual funds that match you and your goals. In Chapter 2 you saw how stocks outperformed bonds and cash equivalents over the past 15 years, but you also learned that the returns on bonds and cash were more consistent and less risky. Look to stocks for growth and to bonds and cash for safety. The more growth-oriented you are, the more you should use mutual funds that invest primarily in stocks. Conversely, the more you lean towards preservation of capital, the more you need to rely on funds that invest in bonds and cash equivalents.

Mutual funds have different mixes of investments depending on their investment objectives. Give some thought to the basic mix of funds you're going to have in your portfolio. It's not enough to decide to put your hard-earned dollars in mutual funds. You have to know which types of funds to use and in what proportion. We'll take this further when we start selecting funds in Chapter 5, but for now, let's go over my guidelines for allocating your assets. The recommendations are given with a range of percentages to account for two important factors:

Each of us is different. Though two people may both consider themselves growth investors, there still can be a big difference in the amount of risk each is willing to take.

Market conditions change. You can be more aggressive than normal when the market is undervalued (you'll see how to find market peaks and valleys in a few pages). When the market is overvalued, you need to pull in your horns.

Setting your investment objectives means balancing risk and reward—fear and greed. Put your own personal stamp on what these words mean. You don't want to risk losing everything any more than you want to be standing on the platform without a ticket when the express train blows through. How can you equate these two conflicting emotions? To start, you must understand risk.

THREE KINDS OF RISK—BUT YOU CAN SIDESTEP TWO

There are three kinds of risk: market risk, default or bankruptcy risk, and sector risk.

Market risk is a fact of life, like the tide coming in each day. Markets—any and every market—fluctuate, and you really can't avoid that unless you don't invest. You can spread your assets among different markets, using both stocks and bonds, but every market will bob up and down. Accept it. It's inevitable.

Default or bankruptcy risk becomes reality when a stock or bond seemingly hits a greased banana peel and slides into oblivion. It can happen; look at the Washington Public Power Supply System (WPPSS) bonds or the Manville, Storage Technology, or Continental Illinois stocks. Catastrophes or bad management can destroy companies or even public agencies. Fortunately, one major advantage of having a portfolio of funds is that this type of risk is almost eliminated. Through the funds, you hold so many stocks or bonds that you really do not have to worry about default or bankruptcy affecting you in a big way.

Sector risk is very simple. If you put your money in the wrong types of investment you miss out. Everything is taking off and your funds are standing still or even moving backwards. In the first nine months of 1987, mutual funds that held a lot of electric utility stocks were poor performers.

The S & P 500 was up more than 37 percent for the period, while many of these funds were up less than 10 percent. For investors in those funds, it was maddening. Every day they heard about another sizeable market move, and their wimpy stocks didn't even budge. On the other hand, when the market crashed in October, those unloved electric utilities were suddenly one of the best-performing sectors.

Spread your investments around. Don't concentrate on one or two sectors of the economy. Don't put all your money in gold funds or bond funds or high-tech funds. In fact, I think most investors would be better off avoiding aggressive growth and sector funds altogether. Using them properly requires nearly perfect timing (if you want to use sector funds, start slowly and cautiously). If you do buy aggressive funds, you should buy the out-of-favor ones. Most investors make the mistake of chasing the "hot" fund. They often catch it just before a big drop. Unless you spend a lot of time following the market, the best bet is a portfolio of diversified mutual funds, which avoids the risk of being in one or two sectors that perform poorly.

Now that you understand risk and the value of diversification, you can work out a menu of funds that is right for you. For each type of fund in the lists below, you'll see a range of percentages. These give you the flexibility to adjust your mix of funds to reflect changing market conditions.

MUTUAL FUND RECIPES SUITED TO YOUR TASTE

Growth (primary): You are willing to accept significant market risk in order to get a high return.

Fully Invested: Full Speed Ahead	Minimum Positions: Batten the Hatches
35% in growth and income funds.	25% in growth and income funds.
60% in growth mutual funds.	25% in growth mutual funds.
5% in money market funds.	50% in money market funds.

Growth (primary) and Income (secondary): You can accept moderate market risk and are willing to accept lower returns in exchange for the reduced risk.

Fully Invested: Full Speed Ahead	Minimum Positions: Batten the Hatches
60% in growth and income mutual funds.	35% in growth and income mutual funds.
20% in growth mutual funds.	0% in growth mutual funds.
15% in bond funds (short term).	35% in bond funds (short term).
5% in money market funds.	20% in money market funds.

Income (primary) and Growth (secondary): You can accept only modest market risk, and you must use some of the cash flow or income for living expenses.

Fully Invested: Full Speed Ahead	Minimum Positions: Batten the Hatches
50% in growth and income mutual funds.	25% in growth and income mutual funds.
40% in bond mutual funds (intermediate).	50% in bond mutual funds (intermediate).
10% in money market funds.	25% in money market funds.

"Fully invested: full speed ahead" means you are very confident about the market trend being strongly positive. In other words, you believe you're early on in a bull market, such as the one that started in August 1982.

"Minimum positions: batten the hatches" describes asset mixes for the times when a bull market is tired and valuation benchmarks are nearing the upper end of their range. A bear market may be coming at any time. There are some who might advocate being 100 percent in cash at market peaks, but that presumes you really can call the market with pinpoint accuracy. Don't be so sure.

HOW TO WIN IN TODAY'S HIGH-RISK MARKETS

Can you succeed in today's volatile environment? Have things become too complex for the average investor? Absolutely not. In fact, solid long-term investments are well within your grasp as a part-time investor. But remember, good investing is simple in theory, more difficult in execution.

Today's "hip" money scorns an investment that lasts more than a few months. Now the accepted wisdom is that you have to trade frenetically to stay on top of things. You have to switch from stock funds to bond funds this week and back to stocks next week. I've heard many "experts" claim the old rules no longer hold, that we're living in a new age where buy and hold strategies won't work. That same tired argument has been used in the past, usually just before a market crash.

Speculative approaches are insidious—they do seem to work, for a while. In a bull market, there are always sectors (high tech, gold, oil) that perform explosively. Certain investments seemingly can do no wrong. They rocket out of the silo and go straight up into space. At times, you've probably looked up at one of those soaring investments 10 miles above everyone else and wondered why you didn't have the sense to strap in and take off with it. Then, after a market crash, you silently thank yourself for being too smart to go with that "obvious" loser.

Out of all the smoke, heat, and ashes of repeated market disasters, you *can* find a few investments or investment styles that have worked well for the past sixty years. These methods also help indicate overheated markets, because they stop working when the market passes the red line. We've all heard the hackneyed phrase "buy low and sell high," but the real question remains "What is high and what is low?" To find the answer, let's check out some time-tested standards of value.

SCOUTING OUT STOCK MARKET PEAKS AND VALLEYS

For any investor it helps to know if the primary trend is up or down—bull or bear. The way to do this is to identify market peaks and valleys. If you know when the market is undervalued or overvalued, you can more easily determine the likely trend. The way to analyze the market's valuation is to compare current statistics to long-term benchmarks or standards for value.

Two important benchmarks are the P/E ratio and the dividend yield of either the Dow or the S & P 500. You can easily look up the current levels for these benchmarks by picking up *Barron's* and going to the "Market Laboratory/Stocks" section. This is usually two or three pages from the end. Look for a small box labeled "Indexes' P/E & Yields." It will show the statistics for last week, the previous week, and one year previous.

Whenever P/Es move in the range of six to eight, you are at or near a bear market low. At the same time, you should see dividend yields at or above six percent.

Market peaks have P/Es in the 18 to 20 range and dividend yields under three percent. In 1987, both of those barriers were reached and exceeded. The fact that a benchmark is passed should be a strong warning telling you there's trouble ahead.

The market regularly moves between extremes. But what do you do when it's somewhere in the middle? By using these benchmark statistics, you can see where the market is, and decide where you think it is heading. From there you can determine how aggressive to be. The best idea when the market is neither high nor low is to remain between the fully invested and minimum positions fitting your particular set of investment objectives. Ride out the dips until the market gets near a historical peak. At that point, pare down your holdings to the minimum positions.

Those who want to go further with market analysis can look at factors such as the price/book value of the stocks in the S & P 500 or the Dow. Book value is calculated by adding corporate assets, subtracting liabilities, and dividing the net total by the number of shares of stock outstanding. This gives book value, or tangible net assets per share. Bear markets can drive stocks prices down close to book value. At market peaks, stocks are usually priced at over two times book value. In 1987, the price/book ratio hit a new high of approximately 2.7 in the months before the October crash.

WATCH THE FEDERAL RESERVE

The actions of the Federal Reserve Board have an enormous impact on interest and the stock and bond markets. Though I don't expect you to spend a lot of time watching the Fed, you should have a working knowledge of what smart mutual fund managers watch. Their basic goal is to determine if the Fed is making money more plentiful and driving interest rates down ("easy money") or taking steps that will force rates up ("tight money"). Generally, higher interest rates or tight money is bad for both stocks and bonds, while lower rates or easy money is good.

If you want a simple, reliable way to track the trend, check 90-day Treasury bill rates. If rates have been trending higher for several months, it indicates the Fed is taking steps to make money tight, and that could ultimately put the market into a tailspin. If this is occurring when the market is at a peak in valuation, watch out. This explosive combination—a high market valuation and tight money—is what led to the crash in October 1987.

PUT IT ALL TOGETHER WITH INVESTMENT STYLES THAT HAVE SURVIVED SIX DECADES OF MARKET VOLATILITY

Let's spend a few minutes analyzing the investment strategies that have transcended the economic booms and busts, the market panics and peaks of the past 60 years. Then we can develop a portfolio of funds. The following are a few of the investment techniques used by many consistently successful mutual fund portfolio managers.

Value: This is a numbers-driven investment approach. It was developed by the legendary investor Benjamin Graham. His most famous pupil, Warren Buffett, has refined the approach and shown, over a very long period, that it can and does beat the S & P 500. Very simply put, Graham was a bargain hunter. He analyzed investments on the basis of their intrinsic value and he used simple, plain vanilla accounting rules to measure value. His goal was to find companies whose assets were worth twice what the stock was selling for.

That sounds pretty simple, right? The hard part comes in two ways. First, it's not always easy to determine the real value of something, be it stock in a company or a piece of real estate. Nor is it always easy to get yourself to buy, even though the numbers are right. Depressed assets always have problems, so you have to learn to pick the cherries and eat around the pits. Many investors have used this style or variations on it. Michael Price and the Mutual Series Fund use this approach, in combination with other techniques. Neuberger & Berman's excellent stock funds—Partners, Guardian, and Manhattan—all put a heavy emphasis on value. Most of the best portfolio managers in the business also use this technique or some variation of it.

Equity-Income: Another way mutual fund portfolio managers identify undervalued stocks is to buy good quality stocks when their dividend yields are high. One practitioner of this philosophy, Roger Newell of the Vanguard Equity Income Fund, compares a stock's current yield with the overall yield of the Standard & Poor's 400 to get a relative yield for that stock. He then compares that relative yield with the stock's historical relative yield. Since he follows only large, well-financed companies, this lets him buy good stocks at favorable prices. Of course, he has to be astute enough to know that the company is simply having short-term problems, not sliding into bankruptcy.

When a solid company's stock plummets, two things happen—one, the P/E goes down, and two, the dividend yield goes up. For example, if IBM is at $150 and its earnings are $7.50, then its P/E is 20 (150 ÷ 7.50 = 20). If the dividend is

$4.40, then the yield is about 3 percent (4.40 ÷ 150 = .03). Assuming earnings and the dividend payout stay constant, when the price drops to $120, the P/E goes to 16 and the yield goes to 3.7 percent.

Many fine companies like IBM stub their toes occasionally. IBM did in 1986, and everyone gave up on it. The stock dropped to $115 per share on all the bad news. A few months later, it hit 169 as an upsurge in earnings occurred. On Black Monday, October 19, 1987, IBM hit another low, at 103. It had fallen, in less than two months, from a high of 175⅞. Within a couple of weeks it shot back up to $122. The extreme differences in price lay not in the company, but simply in the market's perception of it. The market's perception is reflected in a company's stock price and its P/E.

The equity-income approach has been used extensively by many people. Two other equity-income mutual funds are T. Rowe Price Equity Income Fund and Fidelity Equity Income Fund. Both of these have fine records.

Small company stock: This is so simple that most people ignore it. Ask yourself, where does economic growth come from? The answer: small, rapidly growing companies. They provide the bulk of growth, they provide most new jobs, and they develop the innovations that make our lives better. Did IBM market the first personal computer? No. Apple Computer did, when it was a fledgling Silicon Valley start-up.

As a side effect of all this growth, small company stocks far outperform big company stocks over most periods of time. There have been exceptions; for example, the bull market of the 80s was led by the 100 largest companies in the market. But exceptions aside, growth in stock values generally marches along with growth in a business. If you want to grow, buy small company stocks. Stephen Lieber's Evergreen Fund was founded in 1971 to do just this. There are very few pure small-company mutual funds, but most growth and aggressive growth funds invest in small, growing companies as a significant portion of their portfolio.

Besides guiding the choice of which stocks to buy, successful strategies also help mutual fund portfolio managers decide when to sell stocks and buy bonds or money market funds. The best indicators for this are the value and low P/E approaches, which give signals of market peaks and troughs. If a value investor can't find stocks that fit his or her definition of value, then the only answer is to wait—go into cash or buy bonds.

Read any interview Warren Buffett, the legendary Omaha investor, gave in 1986 or early 1987. He said he was simply not buying more stocks, because the market was overvalued. He did the same thing in 1969 and didn't come back in until after the collapse in 1973 and 1974. The key to your investment success is to use mutual funds that develop, and stick with, firm standards for value. When undervalued stocks can't be found, the value-seeking mutual fund portfolio manager moves progressively into cash.

Now that you have a feeling for market trends, you need to develop a portfolio of mutual funds that reflect your investment objectives. Here are examples of successful mutual funds in three categories—growth, growth and income, and income:

GROWTH AND CAPITAL APPRECIATION FUNDS

Fidelity Magellan Fund[1]
Gabelli Asset Fund
Mutual Series Fund[2]
Evergreen Fund
Janus Fund
GIT Special Growth Fund
Manhattan Fund
Pennsylvania Fund
Vanguard World Fund/International Growth
T. Rowe Price International Stock Fund

[1]Charges sales commission.

[2]New names for Mutual Shares (closed), Mutual Qualified (closed) and Mutual Beacon (open but with high minimum).

GROWTH AND INCOME/EQUITY-INCOME FUNDS

T. Rowe Price Equity-Income Fund
Vanguard Equity-Income Fund
Dodge & Cox Stock Fund
Carnegie-Cappiello Trust[1]
Guardian Fund
IAI Stock Fund
Selected American Shares
Trustees U.S. Equity Portfolio

[1]Charges sales commission.

TAXABLE BOND FUNDS

Pacific Investment Management Institutional Trust (high minimum)[1]
Harbor Bond Fund[1]
Vanguard Fixed Income Fund
Neuberger & Berman Limited Maturity

[1]These mutual funds do not have long performance records (both have same portfolio manager), but management is very good.

TAX-FREE MUNICIPAL BOND FUNDS

Neuberger & Berman Municipal Securities Trust
Vanguard Municipal Bond Fund
Stein Roe Managed Municipal Bond Fund
Dreyfus Intermediate Tax Exempt Bond Fund
Fidelity Limited Term Municipals

One final note on these funds. My firm uses many of these mutual funds for our clients, but don't just jump on our bandwagon. This is by no means an exhaustive list. Do your own research and set up your own portfolio of funds based on your personal investment objectives.

INFLATION: LURKING IN THE SHADOWS

Many investors are too conservative, putting their entire portfolio in Treasury bills or certificates of deposit. Instead of a living, growing mix of investments, they end up with a petrified forest. The understandable fear of losing what they have blinds them to a more subtle concern—the grim specter of inflation.

When the rate of inflation is low, it merely nibbles away at your assets, but at higher rates, inflation feasts on your nest egg like a hungry rat. If inflation runs at 5 or 10 percent, your portfolio has to grow by that amount, *after taxes,* just to stay even. Without enough growth, over 10 or 15 years your assets, your net worth, and your spending power could get picked clean. Whether you have many years to work or are retired now, you still have to keep your money growing, or you lose out to inflation.

Even if you are retired and concerned about safety, you should still place some money in stock mutual funds. Though there is risk involved, you need the opportunity for growth. And if you're a growth-oriented investor, don't lose sight of the risks involved.

DON'T FORGET ABOUT MARKET RISK

We talked about three kinds of risk—market, default or bankruptcy, and sector. With a diversified portfolio of mutual funds, you are highly insulated from both default and sector risk, but market risk is unavoidable. Your level of market risk depends on how aggressively you use the different types of mutual funds you invest in, and on general conditions in the stock and bond markets. If stocks are at a low point, even aggressive funds are relatively safe, because all the risk has been let out, like air leaving a tire when it blows. But even conservative funds have substantial risk at market peaks, so you have to be cautious at those times.

Through all the market peaks and valleys, top-performing mutual funds have done a good job of producing solid returns in good markets and preserving capital in bad ones. That's the primary reason the more conservative, balanced mutual funds often outperform more aggressive funds (see Chapter 6 for more on this topic).

How do you put these theories into practice if you don't want to be a full-time research analyst? How can you benefit from these top-performing strategies? By coattailing with mutual funds that use them. The key is to put these strategies to work. Find out what works for you, but get on board funds that use these techniques to build wealth. Though there will be detours and delays, the trip to your financial future will be faster and smoother if you buy a ticket to board high-performance no-load mutual funds. In the next chapter you'll learn how to do that.

5

You Can Find a Fortune in Funds If You Do Your Homework

Searching for great mutual funds is like panning for gold in a mountain stream—you have to wade through a lot of water, sand, and gravel to find a few gleaming nuggets. But before you complain about the effort, let me remind you of that old saw: *If it were easy, everyone would be doing it.* Since few investors do even the most rudimentary research, that makes it easier for you. The information is there, you just have to know how to dig it out.

When most people hear the word *research,* they think of days spent in a high school chemistry lab, playing with foul-smelling vials bubbling away on a Bunsen burner or seemingly endless hours in the musty stacks of a university library. But research doesn't have to be like this.

Suppose you decided to *really* search for gold. Before abruptly plunging into a freezing mountain stream to start panning, you would first scout areas where gold had been found before. You would read books and newspapers and government geological reports to pinpoint the nugget-filled streams. Your eye would automatically search for references to precious metals in magazines, newspapers, and on television. This would become a reflex. Suddenly you'd start seeing reports on gold discoveries, and you'd try to talk with anyone who had ever prospected before. You wouldn't become an instant expert, but in a surprisingly short time you would be knowledgeable about prospecting techniques and gold-rich regions.

That's what I mean by research—close, careful study. In this chapter we'll use these same logical steps to prepare you for successful investing.

I'm sure you've already taken some of these steps on your own; you've read magazines that report on mutual funds and talked to your friends. But chances are you've gotten bogged down. You're overwhelmed by the sheer volume of information. And, if you're like most people, you've done one of two things—picked out a few well-publicized mutual funds, or relied on the advice of a friend or broker.

But investing only by publicity or someone else's advice just doesn't cut it. If you're content with mediocre performance, stop reading and go watch a ballgame. To do better, you must roll up your sleeves, pick yourself up and move off dead center, something most people won't do. In fact, many people plan their vacations more thoroughly than their investments. Why? Because they know they must be organized when that plane takes off. But isn't your money just as time sensitive?

To find mutual fund gold, it's crucial to know where to look. I'm going to show you exactly where and how to do just that. You may enjoy the research—but even if you don't, it's still necessary. Your money, your future, your family deserve better than a few moments of chitchat with your buddy or broker.

Let's review the basics from Chapter 2. They are:

☐ Set clear objectives and guidelines.
☐ Use investments that mirror your objectives.
☐ Coattail with the pros.
☐ Track results, cut losses, and stick with winners.

Take a hard look at Basic Number 3: Coattail with the pros. Until you know who the pros are and how to find them, you can't tap into their brains. So get ready—you are about to go on a voyage of discovery.

START DIGGING AT THE PUBLIC LIBRARY

The first stop is your local public library. Now I know this requires effort; you can't just turn these pages and be entertained, you actually have to do something. You probably haven't been in a library in years. This is where we find out how much desire you have. Can you give up a few hours— that's all I'm talking about—in return for knowing more about mutual funds than most investors? I think you can. In fact, I'm counting on you.

Sure, you could stay home and simply subscribe to a few newsletters or magazines and feel like you're partially doing the job. But in your heart, you know that's not enough. And I'm confident that once you find out how painless it is, you'll be amazed more people don't do their own research. Why do I suggest the library as the first stop? Because a good public library has a vast amount of information on investments. Plus, the library has a trained staff to help you. If you tell them what your goal is, they will suggest other books and periodicals too. So trust me; make a date with your local librarian.

When you walk in the door, you may feel a little out of place. Everyone seems so preoccupied and busy. But remember, your tax dollars are paying their salaries and you have the right to their advice. Exercise it.

At the research or information desk, explain that you want to learn more about mutual funds. You have a list of publications you're going to want, but you also would like to know of other magazines, newsletters, and reference works the library has on the subject. For starters, if you want to be a knowledgeable investor, you need some familiarity with a selection of the following newspapers and magazines:

□ The *Wall Street Journal.*
□ The *New York Times.*

☐ *Investor's Daily.*
☐ *Forbes.*
☐ *Barron's.*
☐ *Business Week.*
☐ *Money.*

This is not an all-inclusive list, nor am I suggesting you read all of these religiously. You should, however, read a few copies of each to find one or two whose method of presenting information appeals to you.

Every weekday morning I read the business section of my local paper, the *San Francisco Chronicle,* and I read the *Wall Street Journal.* I also read the *New York Times* several times a week. Each Monday, I look through *Barron's.* For a quick, irreverent look at Wall Street, I read Alan Abelson's front page column, *Up & Down Wall Street.* Abelson is smart, very funny, and, usually, right on target. *Forbes* comes every two weeks and I love reading it because of the short, pithy articles and its aggressive, muckraking style of journalism. I also read *Business Week* and *Money,* although I scan those more quickly. *USA Today* tends to do quick hits on subjects, but I have seen some good articles there. And *Changing Times* has excellent coverage on mutual fund investing. Once a quarter, *Barron's* prints Lipper Analytical Services' mutual fund performance data plus numerous articles on mutual fund investing. *Forbes, Business Week,* and *Money* also regularly devote issues to mutual funds.

Three excellent mutual fund reference resources are available at public libraries: *Mutual Fund Values, The Handbook for No-Load Fund Investors,* and the *Wiesenberger Investment Company Service.* The next section shows you how you can use Wiesenberger. If you have access to either *Mutual Fund Values* or *The Handbook for No-Load Fund Investors,* turn to Appendixes A and B for more on these.

SHORTCUT TO SUCCESS

Searching for great mutual funds can seem complex, but I'm going to show you a few shortcuts. First, in order to select good funds, you don't have to become an expert in all the details of *each* type of mutual fund. True, many books and magazines go into pages of detail on how government securities funds work or how "junk bond" funds work. You can find complex discussions of the merits of a Japanese stock fund versus a Korean fund. If you're just dying to spend evenings and weekends studying everything from prospectuses to business magazines and books, that's great, but I really don't think it's necessary or even desirable.

That may sound contradictory, but it's the truth. I'm not saying it wouldn't be helpful if you knew the difference between all the categories of bond funds and stock funds. Rather, I'm saying, "First things first."

The blunt truth is that you only have a limited amount of time for investments. An hour or two a week, maybe more, maybe less. From that time you want results—the capital appreciation and income that investments can produce. But let's be realistic; you don't wake up on a Sunday morning and feel a burning desire for an aggressive growth fund or a Ginnie Mae fund. These are the means, not the end. Before you select the means, make sure you know what your end, or goal, is.

When buying a new car, you wouldn't spend your time researching all makes and models from Buicks to Ferraris, station wagons to sports cars. If you wanted a family car, you'd look at three or four makes and models that fit your needs and wouldn't take all your cash. Similarly, mutual funds are vehicles you can use to reach your goals and investment objectives. Focus your research time on those that are likely to get you where you want to go. If your objective is growth, but you put your money in a slow-growth government securities bond fund, then the hours you spent understanding the fund and its Ginnie Mae mortgage-backed bonds and hedging strategies were wasted. Bond funds are generally not growth vehicles. Spend your precious free time studying and focusing on investment essentials, not blind alleys and detours.

IT ALL BOILS DOWN TO FINDING AND STICKING WITH THREE INVESTMENT ESSENTIALS

To manage your investments, you must:

- ☐ Understand your investment objectives.
- ☐ Develop a sound long-term strategy based on sources of objective information.
- ☐ Execute your strategy with patience and emotional control.

Until you have a clear and complete understanding of your own personal investment objectives, you are flying blind. And unless you develop a rational investment strategy, you are bound to remain fogged in. Finally, until you can ignore the constant clatter of the marketplace, you will experience a lot of emotional and *financial* ups and downs with very little forward progress.

FINDING THE STARS IN A CAST OF THOUSANDS

Once you know your objectives, how do you pick the right mutual funds from the thousands in the marketplace? The choices seem overwhelming. But don't focus on individual funds—yet. You're the prospector who wants to pan through the sand and gravel and get down to the gold. Set minimum requirements and discard inferior funds that don't meet that standard. Here are red flags you can use to whittle the cast of thousands down to a manageable number.

Red Flag: No Long-Term Track Record

If a fund doesn't have a record dating back 5 years, forget it. The reason I suggest a 5-year span is to make sure any period you study includes both good and bad markets. You could use a shorter period, if you are careful to go back to the last "bear" market. If you don't want to worry about that, stick with 5 years. This short cut will save a lot of time.

Turn to the section in *Wiesenberger* called "Illustrations of a $10,000 Investment." Pick the "5-Year Summary." Go down the list and write down the names of the top 50 funds in the sections called "Maximum Capital Gains," "Long-Term Growth — Income Secondary," "Growth & Current Income," "Balanced Funds," "Income Funds," and "Specialized and/or International Funds." Don't pay too much attention to *Wiesenberger*'s categories; there are a number of overlapping areas. For example, Ginnie Mae funds are listed under specialized funds, not bond funds. The column to compare is the "Total Value" column, the second from the right.

(I'm sure your eyes may be glazing over a bit as you stare at the columns of names and numbers. But you're not alone; I'm going to walk you through this maze, step by step. You have to fight the tendency to put this off, to read a magazine or go out for coffee. You're like an Alaskan prospector in a freak summer blizzard. If you just keep moving through the subzero weather, there's a blazing fire, hot food, and a shot of brandy up ahead. Your partner is exhausted; he just wants to stop for a few minutes. His feet are numb, and he wants to drop in his tracks and sleep. But you know if the two of you stop now, you may never get going again. So cajole, plead, beg, do whatever it takes to get him going. Lift, drag, or even carry him if you have to, but do whatever it takes to keep moving.)

This section in *Wiesenberger* lets you pick the funds with the top cumulative performance over a long span that includes a serious "bear" market or two.

Funds that invest primarily in stocks are usually the top performers. The performance of bond or income funds generally lags behind that of stock funds, but they still should be selected for their ability to act as an anchor to windward when your portfolio runs into a storm. Look at bond or income funds as a separate category from stock funds. Be careful: Cumulative performance numbers for bond funds will favor high-risk, long-term funds, because the last several years have been favorable for them. To ferret out the best short and intermediate-term bond funds, you must look at those that had a good record of preserving capital in times of high interest rates such as 1979–80–81 or the first three quarters of 1987. Many new short and intermediate funds are just coming out now, so they won't show up in *Wiesenberger*. Several fund groups, among them T. Rowe Price and Neuberger & Berman, have recently started lower-risk short or intermediate-term bond funds.

Once you have 50 mutual funds that meet your minimum requirement—5 years of good performance—you must scrutinize each fund. But first, narrow the field a bit by throwing out funds that have any of the following red flags flying.

Red Flag: Front-End Load or Deferred Sales Charge

Let's eliminate any mutual funds with sales charges and see what that does to the list. You can find this information in the section of *Wiesenberger* entitled "Mutual Fund Panorama." The final column on the left-hand page tells you the sales charge, if any. This will eliminate more than half of the top 50 funds.

Next, start analyzing each of the remaining mutual funds. Think of how hard you would grill your brother-in-law or someone else who wanted to borrow $10,000 from you. Even though the borrower promises you a competitive return, you would demand to know what he was going to do with the money, how he would safeguard your dollars, and how he was planning to pay you back. Though a mutual fund isn't really borrowing money from you, ask the same questions.

We've gotten the cast of thousands down to a much smaller number, but because we're searching for a few great funds, let's make our requirements more stringent.

Red Flag: A 15 Percent or Greater Loss in Any Single Year

There is one exception to this rule, and that concerns periods when the market was down 15 percent or more for the full year. If a fund was around in 1973 and 1974, it probably was down at least 15 percent in one of those years, because the market dropped 14.8 percent in 1973 and another 26.5 percent in 1974.

In checking the 15 percent loss factor, go back to the 1973–74 period to see if the fund was in business and how it performed. You may find it shocking that an otherwise great-looking fund collapsed in that treacherous two-year period. For example, Nicolaus Fund, which has an exceptional record since then, was down 52.7 percent in 1973 and 33.5 percent in 1974. To get the annual performance number for 1973, you will have to ask the librarian for the 1982 edition of *Wiesenberger*.

Lipper Analytical Services reports the *average* stock mutual fund dropped 24.5 percent in October 1987. Many funds sank even further. When you have some funds you're interested in, check out how they performed during market crashes.

But how do you measure risk? One good method is to measure the fund's largest annual loss. This is a way of taking a "worst case" look at a particular fund. To start, turn to *Wiesenberger*'s section called "Management Results: Total Return." Look up the page numbers for the funds you want in the index at the back of the book.

TUDOR FUND NOSEDIVES 25 PERCENT

Look at the Tudor Fund. It has had an excellent track record for many years, but the annual performance numbers don't tell it all. They partially mask the fund's highly volatile record. Tudor was only down a modest 7.2 percent for the full year in 1984. However, it had four successive down quarters beginning July 1, 1983. On a cumulative basis for that period, Tudor was down approximately 25 percent at the end of June 1984. At that point, it pulled out of its nosedive and moved back up, masking much of the poor performance earlier in the year. But many investors, seeing their dollars in the fund drop by 25 percent, pulled out in July and missed the next up move.

Dissecting a fund's track record requires an analysis of the percentage declines on a quarterly or monthly basis. My partner and I do this for our clients, but I am not suggesting you do it unless you loved statistics when you were in school. Though *Wiesenberger* does provide this information, most libraries only have copies going back a couple of years. To go back further, you would have to call each fund and get the quarterly numbers directly from them. If you want to do this, ask for the total return performance on a quarter-by-quarter basis.

DISSECTING FUNDS IS EASIER THAN PANNING FOR GOLD

Look at the section in *Wiesenberger* called "Mutual Fund Descriptions, Charts, and Tables." This section is divided into two segments: full-page summaries for the larger funds, and shorter, less detailed ones for smaller funds. Towards the bottom of the page for bigger funds, you see a chart that shows the cumulative results of the fund's performance. You can eyeball this to see if there were any big dips and when they occurred. Simply by looking at the chart, you can spot a fund with a lot of fluctuations.

A glaring example would be the 44 Wall Street Fund. Pick a date, almost any date, and you will find this fund had volatile performance. An investor who held $136,535 worth of shares at the end of 1983 would have seen his capital shrink to only $55,185 at the end of 1984. This type of volatility jumps right off the page at you when you look at a chart of past performance.

Red Flag: 15 Percent or Greater Cumulative Loss Any Time in the Last 10 Years

To measure the risk of absolute loss in a fund, get out your calculator. You will be measuring the percentage decline from the highest point on the chart to the lowest subsequent point. For example, from the chart, the high point for 44 Wall Street at the end of 1982 was approximately $145,000. The 1985 low was approximately $45,000. So 44 Wall Street had a 69 percent cumulative loss—far more than the 15 percent loss that is enough for a red flag.

When you look at the charts, be careful, because the scale on the left-hand side of the chart varies from fund to fund. Here's the formula to calculate the percentage decline: Divide the low number by the high one and then subtract that fraction from one. This gives you the percentage drop. If this sounds like gobbledygook, here are the numbers for the 44 Wall Street example:

$$\$45,000 \text{ divided by } \$145,000 = .31,$$
$$1 - .31 = .69,$$
$$.69 \times 100\% = 69 \text{ percent.}$$

There are exceptions to the 15 percent cumulative loss rule, just as there were when we were talking about annual percentage drops. Most stock mutual funds were down 15 percent or more in October 1987 because the market was down over 20 percent for the month. The 1973–74 period was another time when almost all funds dropped 15 percent. But for most more normal periods, this red flag will weed out poor performers, like 44 Wall Street Fund, that had big drops in their values—no matter when it occurred in the 10-year period. If digging this out sounds like more work than you want to do, an alternative would be to rely on the risk ratings in the various magazines I've mentioned.

Red Flag: Change in Management or Investment Policies

Go back to the "Management Results: Total Return" section of *Wiesenberger*. Look for those funds that have a double asterisk on the left side of the fund's name. This asterisk means a fund had a significant change in investment policies or management. This probably invalidates the track record. Toss these funds out.

PULLING THE PLUG ON PURITAN

We used the Fidelity Puritan Fund for our clients for several years. Puritan is a conservatively run mutual fund that seeks the highest level of income consistent with preservation of capital. The portfolio is balanced among bonds, stocks, and cash equivalents. The portfolio manager, Francis Cabour, had done a superb job, but in April 1987 he was moved from Puritan to Fidelity Balanced Fund, a similar but much smaller fund. The company brought in Richard Fentin to run Puritan; Fentin had been running the Fidelity Growth Fund since 1983. At the same time, Fidelity added a two percent load or commission to Puritan and started a heavy advertising campaign touting the fund's track record.

At that point we decided to pull the plug on Puritan. Red flags were popping up all over. The veteran portfolio manager had left and the new guy did not have the same level of experience in this style of investing. Plus, the fund was now a load fund and, because of all the advertising, new money was literally coming in by the truckload. Track records are built by specific people—not management committees—so if the top-performing portfolio manager moves on, you should too.

After tossing out funds that have had management changes, look in the "Statistical History" section for annual data on expense ratios. In Chapter 3 you learned about expense ratios. These include most of the usual expenses incurred by a mutual fund in the normal course of operations.

Red Flag: Expense Ratio of More Than 1.5 Percent for Any Fund Over $30 Million in Assets

Anything over 1.5 percent expense ratio is an immediate red flag unless it is a small fund with assets under $30 million. When funds are starting out, they have certain fixed expenses that must be paid no matter what size the fund is. As the shareholders put in more money, these fixed costs go down as a percent of assets.

Fees are important. Don't forget, they come out of your return. I'm not suggesting this be the basis for selection, but it is worth looking at. If a mutual fund has an exceptional record and a high expense ratio is the only red flag, you may consider making an exception.

Small mutual funds generally have higher expense ratios, and this is understandable. Also, stock funds have higher expenses than bond funds. Funds that have a highly active investment style with lots of portfolio turnover will generally have higher brokerage costs than other funds. Exceptions aside, once a fund reaches $50 million or more in assets, its total expense ratio (this does not include brokerage fees) should not be much over one percent.

FAT FEES CAN HURT RESULTS

I recently was contacted by a salesman representing a new mutual fund called the Royce Value Fund, which is run by a well-known mutual fund portfolio manager, Charles Royce. Mr. Royce is also the portfolio manager of the well-known Pennsylvania Mutual Fund. This fund has compiled an outstanding track record. I asked the sales representative about the new fund's expenses—management fee, other expenses, 12b-1 expenses, if any. When I heard the management fee was one percent (usually it is 0.50 to 0.75 percent), I was immediately concerned. When I heard that the fund also has a one percent 12b-1 fee, I stopped right there. I told the fund's representative that a fund that pays out one percent annually for management and another one percent fee for distribution expenses each year is like a swimmer with a weight around the neck—though it's possible to get where you want to go, it's much more difficult. I ruled the fund out on the basis of those two fat fees alone.

Another important area is total net assets. Fidelity Magellan racked up superb performance for years (see page 88) even though it had many billions in assets. Other large funds have also done well. However, a smaller stock mutual fund with $100 million is generally far more maneuverable than one with $10 billion. Conversely, taxable bond mutual funds may actually accrue benefits from being bigger. Their size allows them to profit more readily, given the razor thin margins in U.S. Treasury and government agency bonds.

Read the description in *Wiesenberger* for each of the funds you're looking at. This gives you a quick overview of its investment objectives and policies. This will also give you the asset mix at the time the report was issued, as well as other details. Directly beneath the fund description, *Wiesenberger* has a column labeled "% of Assets in." This gives annual breakdowns of the fund's asset mix among common stocks, bonds and preferreds (preferred stocks), and cash equivalents.

Red Flag: Leverage or Borrowing to Buy Securities (More Than Five Percent)

The fund description will also point to another potential red flag for all but the most aggressive investors: the use of leverage (borrowing money to buy securities). Most mutual funds can borrow up to five percent of their assets to smooth out redemptions, and this is fine. If a fund routinely borrows more than that, it is probably very aggressive.

Eliminating funds based on all these red flags will reduce your list to a few well-run mutual funds. To go further, you need to look at both the prospectus and the statement of additional information. *Wiesenberger* has the phone numbers (often toll-free) for each of the funds, so you can call and request the information.

GRIPPING TALES OF FINANCIAL "WHODUNITS" AND "WHO'S-DOING-IT"

Even if you've only seen a few prospectuses, you know they are pretty boring. Okay, so I was kidding about the gripping tales. But if you want to know where your money is going, you have to read the prospectus—in spite of its weak story line.

Though you've read some prospectuses in your time, you may not be familiar with the statement of additional information. Mutual fund prospectuses used to be much more detailed than they are now. A few years ago, the Securities and Exchange Commission allowed mutual funds to break their prospectuses into two parts:

□ Prospectus.
□ Statement of additional information.

The prospectus has basic information on the fund's investment objectives, management, shareholder services, dividends and tax considerations, the fund's management and investment adviser, brokerage, portfolio turnover, total expense ratio, how to buy shares, minimum investment, how to redeem shares, the names of officers and directors, and other related areas.

The statement of additional information covers some of these areas as well, but in more detail. For example, there is a short paragraph on each of the fund's officers and directors. Since the portfolio manager of many funds is on the fund's board, you can track that person to some extent. The statement should be considered part of the prospectus. Read them together.

The first prospectus you read may seem complicated and confusing. However, after reading five or six, you will be able to move quickly. The information is presented in the same way in each, and you will learn to skip the repetitive sections. Probably the most important information you can get from the prospectus and statement of additional information is a clear concept of the fund's investment objectives. Don't lightly dismiss this part of the research. It's your chance to get acquainted with the funds you'll be entrusting with your cash.

In addition to the prospectus and the statement of additional information, you should review a fund's annual, quarterly, and semiannual reports. From these you can see the specific investments held by the fund. You will also receive some commentary from the fund's president or chairman (more on how to use the quarterly reports in Chapter 7).

KEEP THE FAITH

Now that you have a list of several no-load funds with solid long-term track records and reasonable expense ratios, you probably wonder, "Am I on target?" You may think, "How could my limited knowledge possibly stack up against that of experts?" But don't lose faith; if you have done the work up until now, you know more than you give yourself credit for. And if you stay with me, you will know more than most brokers or financial planners. I know it's hard to believe, but I doubt if one broker or financial planner out of ten would make this kind of effort even though he or she is advising people where to place their life savings (see Chapter 8 for more on this).

Here are two more sources of good information on mutual fund investing:

The Mutual Fund Factbook ($2.00)
The Investment Company Institute
1600 M Street N.W.
Washington, DC 20036

The Individual Investor's Guide to No-Load Mutual Funds ($19.95)
American Association of Individual Investors
P.O. Box 10224
Chicago, IL 60610

Two excellent mutual fund reference books are *Mutual Fund Values* and *The Handbook For No-Load Fund Investors*. Turn to Appendixes A and B for more on how to use these.

Having access to the best sources of information won't help you a bit unless you use them. Make an appointment with yourself right now and go down to your public library. Get started even if you only have an hour. Taking control of your financial future won't seem so intimidating once you get started.

One technique you can use for motivation is to tell your family, spouse, friend, or relatives what you are doing. Tell them your goal is to develop a working knowledge of mutual funds and then to use them to build your (and their) wealth. Doing this will increase your personal commitment because you will have made your goal public. You will be less likely to procrastinate and more likely to build wealth and financial security with a solid portfolio of top performing funds.

TRUE CONFESSIONS: GOOD FOR THE SOUL

Now I have a confession to make. The research methods we've just gone over are quite different from those my partner and I use for our clients. I'm not trying to hold anything back, I'm simply reducing the statistical tests we use to a workable step-by-step procedure based on the resources readily available to you. It's not practical to suggest you look at everything we do. You don't have the data, or the time to figure out how to use it.

We also use a number of new mutual funds, although one of my red flags was the lack of a long-term track record. In the past few years, hundreds of new mutual funds have sprung up. Occasionally, a new one catches our eye because it is run by an investment firm with a great record. One of the funds I mentioned in Chapter 4 falls into that category—Vanguard Equity Income Fund. Although the fund itself does not have a long record, its investment adviser does have an excellent record.

We also use the Pacific Investment Management Institutional Trust, another new fund. This fund is run by Pacific Investment Management, the Newport Beach, California, investment advisory firm. The firm manages over $20 billion and has an outstanding record managing bond portfolios.

So, even though I don't always live by the rules I set for you, I have good reasons for changing them. Jack Nicklaus may say in an instruction book, "Never try to cut the corner of a dogleg on a long par five, and never try to shoot over a large tree," but he may do those very things in a tournament. He's a pro, and he works at it every day. For every rule, there are always a few exceptions. We make exceptions only when we have good reasons. We also watch funds more closely than you will be able to. Either my partner or I talk to the portfolio managers of the funds we use at least once every three months when things are calm, and more often in turbulent markets. So unless you want to become a full-time analyst and investment adviser, stick to the guidelines I've given. They work.

SEVEN RED FLAGS THAT MAY BE FLYING IN YOUR FACE

To review, the red flags I've discussed are:

- ☐ No long-term track record.
- ☐ Front-end load or deferred sales charge, high 12b-1 fees.
- ☐ A 15 percent loss in any single year.
- ☐ Change in management or investment policies.
- ☐ A 15 percent cumulative loss any time in the last 10 years.
- ☐ Expense ratio of more than 1.5 percent for any fund over $30 million in assets.
- ☐ High leverage (borrowing) to buy securities.

FIVE GREEN LIGHTS THAT SAY FULL SPEED AHEAD

If you want a summary of what you *are* looking for, here are green lights to guide you.

- ☐ A 5-year track record performance that equals or exceeds market indexes.
- ☐ Investment policy you understand and agree with.
- ☐ Performance that beat indexes in last bear market.
- ☐ Stable management team.
- ☐ Reasonable cost structure.

Don't forget, if you keep searching in the right places, you will soon find mutual fund gold. To find great funds, dig out the information at your public library. They have all the prospecting tools you need. Use the red and green flags to help you locate the few great funds.

INTERVIEW: CHARLES SCHWAB
Found a Path to Success and Never Veered

Charles Schwab is a living legend among investors. More than anyone, he is the father of discount stock brokerage. Schwab symbolizes a quiet revolution—a radical new direction in the business of financial services. It's not just because he's a discount broker; there are many of them—Quick and Reilly, Fidelity Investments, Olde Discount, Jack F. White, and many more. No, it's because Schwab is a radical, a zealot. He's out to change the world and, not incidentally, make a lot of money doing it. And he's done just that.

The Charles Schwab Corporation is an independent company after four years as a subsidiary of the troubled giant Bank of America. Public investors now own a piece of the firm, although most of them wish they had waited until after the October 1987 crash to buy the stock. After being issued at $16 per share, it traded as low as $6 a few weeks later. During that same period, investors were criticizing his firm because it was unable to handle the enormous volume of phone calls and of buy and sell (mainly sell) orders on Black Monday, October 19.

Schwab, whose perennially boyish face we see from time to time in every financial publication from *Money* to the *Wall Street Journal,* started out with everything going his way. He grew up in California's Sacramento Valley, the son of a county district attorney. After high school, where he was a B+ student and captain of the golf team, he went on to Stanford University. After he graduated with a master's degree in business administration, he went to work for Foster Investment Services and by age 23 was a vice president.

Schwab thought he was hot—it seemed he was on his own personal fast track.

But working for someone else wasn't good enough; Schwab wanted his own firm. This step marked the beginning of 13 years of Job-like trials before he made it to the Promised Land. His new investment firm, Mitchell, Morse, & Schwab, nearly went broke two years after he founded it in 1962.

In 1967 he started a no-load mutual fund called Investment Indicators that became an immediate success. But it soon ran into regulatory problems with the state of Texas. Then, while bureaucrats inflicted the Torture of a Thousand Forms, Schwab's fund gasped and died under the weight of paperwork.

But Schwab's trials weren't over yet. In 1974, he founded Charles Schwab & Company with a little help from his uncle and a few friends. Once again, he stumbled. At that time his company was just another brokerage firm on the street. His firm didn't really find its niche until May 1, 1975—the day commissions on all stock exchanges became fully negotiable—but then it took off like a Saturn rocket, and it's still moving fast.

Today, Schwab's firm has 111 offices in over 100 cities around the country. The firm serves over 1.3 million active customer accounts and is adding more at the rate of 25,000 per month. But Schwab isn't satisfied with his success. Remember, he's a zealot. He wants to help people invest more rationally, more cost-effectively. Recently, he created a new service called the Mutual Fund Marketplace,® the original source for buying and selling no-load mutual funds. Schwab spent over $2 million setting it up even though people said he was nuts. Now, the Mutual Fund Marketplace does $200 million in transactions per week. Schwab believes every investor should own some good, no-load mutual funds. He does himself.

Another Schwab innovation is the Equalizer™, a trademarked piece of personal computer software to help investors make and track investments more easily. With this program investors can actually tap into Schwab's system and place orders to buy or sell over their own personal computer. Schwab has also put out an excellent book for the ordinary investor, *How To Be Your Own Stockbroker* (Macmillan Publishing Co.).

Brouwer: Can an ordinary investor do well on his or her own?

Schwab: Yes, if he or she is willing to put in the effort and learn the fundamentals of investing.

Brouwer: What are some of those fundamentals?

Schwab: First, markets are not logical, they're emotional. The emotional and psychological ingredient is the overwhelming force in the markets. Second, markets move in broad trends, that, with a little effort, investors can understand and profit from. Third, diversify your investments. Whether you're buying individual stocks and bonds, mutual funds, or anything else, you should diversify. Fourth, don't gamble with money you can't afford to lose. If you want to put a small amount in a flyer or two, that's okay. But don't put a big chunk of your money into a highly risky investment. Finally, get a second opinion. Don't make any investment based just on a broker's advice.

Brouwer: What is the most important tip you can give the newer investor?

Schwab: Probably the most important concept to realize is that investments do go up and down; there are bull markets and bear markets. And you, the investor, will have some wildly gyrating emotions when the market soars or falls down in a heap. Greed grabs you in a bull market and fears pull you down when the market crashes. As human beings, we respond to those emotional tugs in strange, often inappropriate, ways. To avoid reacting badly, you must plan beforehand what you are going to do with your money in different market climates. Over and over, I see people sell after a steep decline. When they do, they're out of the market for the next upswing.

Brouwer: What else is important?

Schwab: Investing is a long-term project. The big investment returns come from compounding a good return over a long period. The most powerful compounding effect comes from mutual funds that buy growth stocks, not bonds or money market funds.

Brouwer: What's the first step an investor should take?

Schwab: Learn. Spend time studying investments. The more you study and learn, the better an investor you'll be.

Brouwer: Let's talk about how an investor should begin thinking about his or her investment objectives. For example, a 30-year-old probably has different objectives than a 60-year-old.

Schwab: That's right. I call it life cycle investing. In other words, a young person has different investment objectives than a middle-aged businessman. And a retired person usually has objectives that are different from either of the other two. The younger you are, the better it is to start investing. You have that much more time to compound. But there are other concerns too. If you are getting involved in the market for the first time at age 50, certainly you shouldn't take the same kind of risk that you would at age 35.

Brouwer: Are there any basics, fundamentals that apply to each of the three life cycle groups?

Schwab: Sure. First, everyone needs to keep several months' expenses in a money market fund or bank account. If you have a family or your own business, you definitely should have term life insurance.

Brouwer: Term insurance, rather than whole life?

Schwab: Yes. People should buy annual renewable term life insurance. The life insurance industry has promoted the ridiculous notion that you should tie investments and insurance together. This is absurd. Unbundle the two and buy straight insurance and do your investing on your own. You'll be happier, you'll get the coverage you need at a reasonable cost, and you won't be helping insurance companies and their agents get fat off your dollars.

Brouwer: What are some other basics common to each of the three life cycles?

Schwab: Setting up and funding an Individual Retirement Account (IRA) or any other tax-deferred retirement plan you're allowed to contribute to.

Brouwer: What else?

Schwab: Diversification. Don't put all your eggs in one place. I really believe it is important to use no-load mutual funds. For people under 50, you should use growth funds. Just one mutual fund will give you a piece of 20 to 50 different stocks. With that kind of diversity, no single stock going down can hurt you that much. You will get access to stocks you never would have bought on your own, because the fund has professional managers who spend all day looking for bargains. That's far more time than most investors would spend.

Brouwer: Do you personally buy no-load funds? If so, why?

Schwab: Yes, I do. A good no-load mutual fund is one of the best investments you can make—it has it all. I use them and I think every smart investor should have money in several of the best mutual funds he or she can find.

Brouwer: What types of investments should people stay away from?

Schwab: Tax shelter deals, highly speculative things like commodities and precious metals.

Brouwer: So you don't recommend gold or silver?

Schwab: No, unless it's a diversified gold mutual fund.

Brouwer: No gold or silver bars?

Schwab: The high cost of storage, insurance, the lack of dividends or interest, all these make so-called treasure chest investments unworthy of the name investment.

Brouwer: Can someone with $50,000 or less do well buying individual stocks, or should they use mutual funds?

Schwab: Generally, they will do better with mutual funds.

Brouwer: What is the Mutual Fund Marketplace, and why did you start it?

Schwab: The Mutual Fund Marketplace is a service that allows our customers to buy hundreds of no-load and low-load mutual funds within their Schwab brokerage account. And they can buy a fund with one phone call. Our business is making investing easier and more efficient. Now, the investor has a broad selection of mutual funds to choose from, he or she can buy or sell on the telephone. Also, those who want to be more aggressive can buy on margin. And we have a convenient record-keeping system that has all your fund information on one statement.

Brouwer: At first, you had no competition; now I see Fidelity Investments, and probably others, are following your lead. Did you simply alert them to a good opportunity?

Schwab: It is a good opportunity. And I view imitation as a form of flattery.

Brouwer: You've had some operational glitches, growing pains. Are those behind you now?

Schwab: Yes. There were a few learning and growing pains. The Mutual Fund Marketplace is new and we did have some processing problems early on, but I'm confident those are behind us now.

Brouwer: What about market timing? Investors are bombarded with claims about calling the market. Does it really work?

Schwab: In a broad sense, yes it does. In other words, I believe you can see broad trends in the market. I think you can determine if we're in a bull market or a bear market.

Brouwer: How can you pick up on these trends?

Schwab: By studying the general movement of the markets and becoming familiar with the cyclical nature of the market. Also, you need to study interest rates and the money supply. Look at the lists in *Barron's* or the *Wall*

Street Journal showing the number of stocks hitting new highs and new lows. If you see many more new highs than lows, then you're probably well along in a bull market. Look at market volume on the New York Stock Exchange. If it's high, then that's another sign of an extended bull market.

Brouwer: There are many services that try to predict whether the market will be up or down over the next few months. Does this make sense?

Schwab: No. While you can determine broad trends, it's impossible to correctly pick short-term swings in the market with any accuracy.

Brouwer: What about foreign investing?

Schwab: Any observer of recent events would have to agree that we must become more international in our thinking. At least 50 percent of the world's equity market is outside of the U.S. We would be foolish to ignore this completely. At the same time, investors have to realize foreign markets are less regulated than our own. In addition, foreign investments bear the risk of currency fluctuations as well.

Brouwer: What's the best way to do this?

Schwab: Well, some foreign stocks such as Sony, Royal Dutch, and others are listed on the New York Stock Exchange. There are also American Depositary Receipts (ADRs), which are foreign stocks that have an agreement to hold shares in U.S. banks. If you are willing to put in a lot of time or if you have a special expertise in foreign investments, you can buy stocks directly. But most investors would be better off buying an international mutual fund—one that specializes in foreign investments.

Brouwer: Why are so many mutual funds going load recently?

Schwab: Salesmanship. It gives brokers something to do and the mutual funds consider it a quick way to get a lot of money under management. Personally, I think someone buying a load fund is very foolish.

Brouwer: What about tax shelters?

Schwab: Probably the safest tax shelter is real estate. But it's important to stress that the details of each investment are different. And it's critical that you go in only on conservatively structured programs. For example, the more borrowing there is in an investment, the higher the risk. Also, most tax shelters are limited partnerships, and these often take 20 to 25 percent off the top for commissions and start-up costs. That makes it very hard for the investor to make money.

Brouwer: What are some recent examples of investments you've made?

Schwab: In early 1982, I bought several good growth-oriented mutual funds. Even though I was a bit early, in August and September those mutual funds took off.

Brouwer: Why did you buy mutual funds?

Schwab: For the same reasons I think every investor should own no-load mutual funds. Professional management. The investor has expert selection of investments and full-time management of those investments once selected. An investment in a mutual fund will give the investor far more diversification than most people would be able to obtain efficiently. And if investors use no-load funds, they keep their costs at a very reasonable level. Mutual funds are the most highly regulated investment, so investors are protected against fraud. It's also easy to select funds that meet with your needs as an investor.

Brouwer: Which funds did you select?

Schwab: Founder's Special, Sherman, Dean, and DFA Small Company Fund.

Brouwer: Why those particular funds?

Schwab: They had fine track records, and though the funds have different investment objectives, their individual strategies matched what I wanted to accomplish.

Brouwer: That was back in 1982. What about recent investments?

Schwab: I'm mainly involved in my company and in some real estate. In my Individual Retirement Account, I have concentrated on five mutual funds. Columbia Growth, Stein Roe Special, Partners Fund, and Twentieth Century Growth: these funds mainly invest in domestic investments. I also own Explorer II and Scudder International, which invest in overseas markets. As the market gets higher, I may shift some cash out of growth funds and move into more conservative, balanced mutual funds.

Brouwer: Changing the topic a bit, strong emotions seem to have a negative impact on investment results. When people get excited or depressed, it causes them to make bad decisions. How have you learned to control emotion in investing?

Schwab: As I said before, fear and greed are the dominant emotional factors in the investment markets. Either one can cause serious problems. I learned to control these emotions the hard way by making mistakes. Primarily it boils down to going your own way, making your own decisions. And finally, you need to be a survivor—to be resilient. Even though you will make mistakes, you have to keep coming back.

Brouwer: How can others profit from your experience?

Schwab: By focusing on the key concepts we've been talking about and applying them to their personal situation.

Brouwer: Were there times in the early years of Charles Schwab & Company, or even earlier, with the failure of your mutual fund, were there times when you despaired of being successful?

Schwab: Are you kidding? Sure. Many times. Fortunately, I was lucky. I had all my money in the business and I had nowhere to go but straight ahead.

Brouwer: What helped you survive the hard times?

Schwab: An instinct for survival—for shaking off rejection. Being resilient. Not accepting failure. Looking at insoluble problems as opportunities. Now, I'm talking both as a person, as an investor, and as a businessman.

Brouwer: Can the same qualities help other investors?

Schwab: I'm convinced that if you hope to succeed, you have to have a burning desire to overcome obstacles—to survive the hardships and win.

This is how one guy, Charles Schwab, did win—against all odds. Who would have thought he could go head to head against the biggest brokers and win? But he did. He ran his business the way you should handle your investments. He invested for the long run and occasionally had to accept a loss. But he never gave up.

Let's recap four important points Schwab made. First, the investment markets are not logical, they're emotional. They move in broad, discernible trends—up or down. Second, make sure you diversify, and don't gamble with money you can't afford to lose. Third, Schwab stressed his belief that a good no-load mutual fund is one of the best investments you can make. He uses them, and he believes in them. Finally, he advised that, if you want growth, you must invest in mutual funds that buy stocks.

6

Mythbusting: High Risk Seldom Equals High Return and Don't Let Anyone Tell You Differently

High-risk investing is like the Indianapolis 500. The winner gets to kiss a beauty queen, and the loser goes home in a tow truck, if he's lucky, or an ambulance, if he's not.

Professionals race Indy for two reasons—the chance to win and the thrill of the competition. The risk of losing it all doesn't faze them. But as an investor, how would you feel about losing everything? Could you get up from a crushing defeat and keep moving without losing your nerve? If your answer is no, then avoid high-risk investments.

Since shortly after gorillas started walking on two feet, pseudo–wise men have solemnly preached the gospel, "You must take big risks to get big rewards." And frankly, if you want to make a million overnight, that's still true. You have to put all your money on the line and roll the dice. But I don't think that's your goal. I think you want a steady return over the years and you also want to be able to sleep at night.

SAFE AND STEADY DOESN'T MEAN LIFE IN THE SLOW LANE

But are you really giving up that much? If you pass up risky investments, does that mean you have to go from a 200-mph Indy racer to a 55-mph Chevy? No way. What you give up is "action." The Indy racers are there to win, but most of them know the odds are against them. The truth is they'd race anyway, even if there were no money involved. Some people just crave action, thrills, chills, and spills. But the best investments aren't exciting gambles, they're mundane, almost boring, vehicles that can grow at 15 percent a year— a little more in good years, less in bad ones.

Many investors scoff at a 15 percent return. They want more—much more. The takeover deal. The hot tip on pork bellies going up explosively because McDonald's is coming out with a pork burger. But most hot tips are really stale news items that won't make you, or anyone else, rich. The high-risk investor doesn't care, because he wants action, excitement. That craving, though bad for him, is good for you, because trigger-happy speculators provide opportunities for patient, long-term investors.

Let's be honest. Now and then a high-risk investor does make it big. Look at the players in takeovers or people who put money in fledgling companies like Apple Computer. If you're smart or lucky, preferably both, you can do very well. Speculators can make several hundred percent on one investment when they're right. In these cases high risk and high return go together. But the investors who pull off the big coups are usually fanatics. That's what it takes. Are you willing to make investing your life's work? Don't waste your time and fritter away your money chasing that dream unless you are willing to make the commitment to work as hard at investing as professional athletes do at their obsession.

Amateurs can make a killing, but it happens about as often as a weekend racer's winning at Indianapolis. Even if he could find an Indy-type race car and a crackerjack crew, he wouldn't be able to handle it. If sudden wealth is your dream, or your obsession, you are likely to be disappointed.

As a long-term investor, you don't have to give up that much. Remember the tortoise and the hare. If you maintain a portfolio of top mutual funds and you're patient and not greedy, you'll be amazed at the results.

JUST THE FACTS, PLEASE

In 1990, my partner and I did some research to compare the performance of lower-risk growth and income mutual funds, versus aggressive growth, or high-risk, funds over the 21-year period from 1968 through 1989. We wanted the facts, not just our, or anyone else's, opinion. To accomplish this, we used two indexes. The first covered over 100 growth and income funds, and the second was made up of more than 100 aggressive growth funds. We studied the data for that period (supplied by CDA Technologies, Inc.) to see which type of fund had produced higher returns. In the study we found that the more conservative growth and income funds had outstripped high-risk funds over the entire 21-year period we studied.

What's more, when we factored in the higher risks incurred by the fast-track, aggressive growth mutual funds in their flat-out quest for super-performance, we found they often spun out of control; investment returns sputtered. At the same time, the slower but steadier growth and income mutual funds passed them by and kept the lead.

For example, in July 1983, eleven months into the bull market that started in August 1982, the aggressive growth funds went into a prolonged nosedive, led by the collapse of high-technology stocks. Remember the Tudor Fund example from Chapter 5. Tudor's big drop happened during this period. In fact, most aggressive funds, their portfolios bulging with volatile high-technology stocks, plummeted over 20 percent, while the S & P 500, probably the stock market's best thermometer, was down just under 5 percent.

During the same period—July 1983 through June 1984—growth and income funds matched the S & P 500 as they dropped less than 5 percent.

This dramatic difference in performance between the two categories of mutual funds was not a freak accident or a fluke. A decade earlier—1973 to 1974—when the S & P 500 plunged a dizzying 37 percent in two years, the go-for-big-growth aggressive funds took an even steeper dive.

AGGRESSIVE FUNDS PLUNGE MORE THAN 50 PERCENT!

As a group, aggressive funds dropped more than 50 percent in 1973–74. The more conservative growth and income mutual funds, while not immune to what was then the worst market crash since the Great Depression, fell 33 percent on average.

In recent years, the same pattern has prevailed—over most periods, growth and income funds performed as well or better than aggressive funds, but with much less risk. From January 1980 through December 1989, on average, growth and income funds returned over 15 percent per year, while aggressive funds earned less than 14 percent per year.

DEMISE OF THE RISK/REWARD MYTH

The scenario described above repeated itself over and over in our study. In fact, there were few periods when aggressive growth funds topped growth and income funds. So much, in our view, for the risk/reward myth.

What does this mean to you? If you invested $10,000 in an average growth and income fund in mid-1983, you would have seldom seen a loss in the account, and by the end of 1989 would have owned shares worth $22,900. If your hotshot, Porsche-driving neighbor put $10,000 in an average aggressive growth fund at the same time, his account would have immediately begun to sink and wouldn't have come up for air for 12 months. At the bottom, his account would have only been worth $8,300, and at the end of the period, it would have been worth $17,000. True, he would have made money, but he would surely have wondered if it was worth all the trouble.

But why does the risk/reward myth still exist? Two reasons: First, many people who work for investment firms are really speculators themselves, not long-term investors. They love the "action" of daily trading, and this is what they often recommend to clients. Many investors are also *closet* speculators, who get bored if their latest buy doesn't move quickly enough.

No matter what "sure thing" someone offers you, there is no way to get rich quick—unless you win the state lottery or hit it big in Las Vegas or Atlantic City. And you know what those odds are. Impatience is a cardinal sin that snuffs out many promising investments before they have time to perform.

Does this mean you should only use growth and income funds? Not necessarily. It all depends on your objectives. There were several periods when aggressive growth funds turned in awesome performances. Aggressive growth funds and growth funds can add a lot to your total return if you use them carefully, with respect. But if you do invest in aggressive growth mutual funds, you have to be very concerned and knowledgeable about the stock market cycle.

If you are intrigued by the concept of moving in and out, or "timing" the market with aggressive funds, you should investigate the various mutual fund newsletters. Most libraries have one or more reference books of newsletters, either *The Oxbridge Directory of Newsletters* or *The Newsletter Directory*. Use the reference books and check out all the interesting ones. Most newsletters will gladly send you a sample issue or two. After you've done your homework, pick one that you like best.

You will find that most mutual fund newsletters do some form of market timing based on analysis of a number of statistics or technical market indicators such as volume, the number of stocks up or down, most active stocks and moving averages of the various indexes. Conclusions drawn from this analysis form the basis of their buy and sell decisions.

Everyone who engages in this work routinely claims great success, but most have little to back up their claims. However, the following two newsletters have had their moments.

Dick Fabian's *Telephone Switch Newsletter*
P.O. Box 2538
Huntington Beach, CA 92647

Jay Schabacker's *Mutual Fund Investing*
7811 Montrose Road
Potomac, MD 20854

If you do use a market timing newsletter, you will probably be encouraged to use aggressive mutual funds. These types of funds are wonderful in bull markets and abysmal in bear markets. Timers rely on their technical analysis to get you out of the market before a big drop occurs.

As an example, Dick Fabian told his readers to get out of their funds just before the collapse on October 19, 1987. He made the call on Thursday, the 15th of October. The first, and last, trading day before the crash was Friday, the 16th. If you were on vacation and missed the call by one single day, you would have been fully invested in aggressive funds during Monday's 22.6 percent stock market collapse. Ask yourself if you can live with those razor-thin margins for error.

No matter what your investment goals are, in order to meet them you have to learn patience. If you're in a hurry or driven by greed, you will probably get in trouble. But if you do keep your emotions in check, you will find it easier to build steadily and surely for your future.

Don't get caught in the speed-burner mentality that prizes immediate riches. Think about it; even if you got a 100 percent return this year, would it make that much of a difference in your lifestyle? If a driver at Indy wrecks his car, the corporate sponsor will roll out another one. Sure it costs money, but they just add it to their advertising budget. If you crash your investment vehicle, it's going to take a lot of time to make it back, and time is one thing none of us has enough of.

INTERVIEW: PETER LYNCH
One Up on Wall Street

As we were going to press, Peter Lynch announced his retirement as portfolio manager of Fidelity Magellan Fund. Magellan's superb performance over the years stemmed largely from the innovative investment principles, strategies, and techniques Lynch pioneered during his 13 years at Fidelity. The following provides rare insights into the thought process of a brilliant investor. His approach helped him out- pace most other mutual funds as well as major market indices such as the Standard & Poor's 500. Knowing how Lynch thinks could help you in your search for the next Magellan.

Fidelity Magellan Fund is probably the best-known yet least understood mutual fund in history. The financial press agrees that Magellan "was" a great mutual fund but is now merely a good one. True? Let's take a hard, close look at portfolio manager Peter Lynch and his performance record to find out the truth.

It's no secret that Magellan's early track record was simply spectacular. For the years 1979 through 1981, it outper- formed the Standard & Poor's 500 Stock Index by an average of 30 percent per year. Phenomenal. But the fund was very small in those early years—$107 million in assets by 1981. And it was closed to new investors.

When the fund reopened to new investors in 1981, it also added a three percent front-end commission. Obviously, Fidelity's crafty management knew they had a good thing going and that a sales charge would probably not deter investors. They were right on both counts.

The Magellan Fund soared in 1982, outracing the S & P 500 by over 26 percent in that one year alone. Investors shoveled money into the fund and net assets ballooned to $458 million. More and more investors discovered Magellan, and by the end of 1984 assets were almost $2 billion.

Suddenly, many Wall Street commentators and press pundits decided that Lynch had peaked. Their rationale: A mutual fund this large could no longer outperform market averages. With over 1,000 stocks in the portfolio, they scoffed, Lynch couldn't possibly keep a hot hand. And even Peter Lynch would concede it is harder to beat the averages with billions than with the $107 million he had in 1981.

So what happened? In 1984, Magellan was the largest mutual fund with $2 billion. By 1989 assets had swollen to more than $12 billion, yet year after year Magellan outperformed the S & P 500.

For the five years ending in December, 1989, the S & P 500 grew 152 percent. Lipper Analytical Services reports the average equity mutual fund underperformed the market average with a total return of 110 percent for those five years. How did Magellan compare? Its total return was 195 percent, nearly double the average equity fund. Pretty nifty moves for a big guy when the pressure was on.

How does he do it? Lynch's investment style is very simple in theory, much harder in practice. He buys stocks with plenty of potential for capital appreciation. All types. Growth stocks, cyclical stocks, big ones, little ones—about 1,400 in all. He does not try to outguess short-term market movements by moving in and out. He's gutsy, committed, and remains essentially fully invested at all times.

Many of his most successful investments were either obscure or unpopular when he bought in. In 1982, when events looked bleak for Chrysler Corporation, Lynch bought the stock at $6. Chrysler stock soared over the next several years. Yet it wasn't until Chrysler cracked the $30 barrier that less adventurous money managers bought in.

That just may be why he has consistently beaten other mutual funds. He thinks for himself and ignores the so-called accepted wisdom. He trusts his instincts, his hard work ethic, and the Fidelity organization that gives him the freedom to act decisively. Indeed the average equity mutual fund would do well to learn a lesson from Lynch's long and successful record.

His recent book, *One Up On Wall Street,* was his first-person account of his stockpicking philosophy. But what does he really think about mutual fund investing? I wanted to know.

Brouwer: What's the difference in what you do running Magellan with $12 billion compared to 1981 when you had only $107 million?

Lynch: It's just the same. I have the same size staff I had back then. When I buy a stock like Merck or Chrysler, I go visit them. I talk to them on the phone. Although we do have more analysts than we had 15 years ago, I still visit the companies myself. When I had 25 percent of my fund in autos, I visited all the auto companies. When I had 25 percent in insurance, I visited all the insurance companies. You can't rely on somebody else. If you do, you're not going to have the results you want.

Brouwer: How can you follow 1,400 stocks with the same size staff you had for 150?

Lynch: Even though I may own 1,400 stocks, just 200 of them make up three quarters of the fund's assets. So I am doing a hell of a lot of work on those 200 stocks. I have hundreds of stocks that all together make up only about two percent of the fund's assets. But those are there because I want to keep my eye on them.

Brouwer: Is managing Magellan as much fun as it was 10 years ago?

Lynch: It's more rewarding, but I couldn't say it is as much fun. When you're the biggest, many people want to predict your downfall. They dump all over you at the first sign of lagging performance.

Brouwer: That's a bit unreasonable, since over the past five years you've outperformed 95 percent of all equity funds. To use a golf analogy, in the early years of the fund you shot rounds of 68 when others were scoring 80 or higher. Now, you're shooting 75 and they're still around 80.

Lynch: So now we get asked, what's wrong with Magellan?

Brouwer: That's a very good point. That is the bittersweet aspect of the enormous success you've had. To switch gears a bit, let's talk about a little-known aspect of your success with the fund—your willingness to make big bets, to concentrate a large portion of the fund's assets in one industry group.

Lynch: Many portfolio managers will be really excited about an industry group—say insurance. What they'll do is put three percent of their fund in insurance stocks. Whereas if I'm really excited I might put 15–20–25 percent in one area. I've had 25 percent in autos, 25 percent in financial stocks, 16 percent in banks. I've made huge bets and they have paid off as the record shows.

Brouwer: On a more basic level, Magellan Fund has always been devoted to stocks. Why do you stay fully invested through all the ups and downs in the market?

Lynch: First of all, I don't want to second guess the shareholder. I assume that they have already decided to be in the stock market; that's why they bought the fund. They have made the asset allocation decision. This way they can be confident that if the market goes up, I am going to be there with them. Secondly, I *would* move out of stocks and into cash if every stock I found was overpriced. But ever since I've been in the business, I've been able to find what I thought were reasonably priced or undervalued stocks.

Brouwer: You are talking to an investor who says, "I want capital appreciation and I have money to invest for 20 years, but aren't stock mutual funds too risky?" What would your answer be?

Lynch: People think the stock market is a big gamble. It's megabucks or nothing at all, like a lottery ticket. But if you select a good stock mutual fund and they have done their job and are conscientious, they'll have a few mistakes, but those will be more than made up by the 5 and 10 baggers.

Brouwer: Five and 10 baggers?

Lynch: Stocks that go up 5 and 10 times.

Brouwer: Because your fund remains fully invested most of the time, you do suffer when the stock market drops. What would you say to someone who feels a sense of panic? Say, for example, they bought into Magellan just before the market dropped in 1987?

Lynch: I would tell them you just have to understand that this is going to happen. And when it happens, the climate will be very negative. You'll be hearing disturbing things in the newspaper, magazines, on television. You may hear people you regard as intelligent say things are going to get much worse, in effect, the end of the world is here. This happened in 1982, again in 1984, and certainly in 1987.

Brouwer: On the other hand, when the market is getting overheated, the news will be almost uniformly positive.

Lynch: Sure. Normally, stock market declines occur in a climate of pessimism. And market blowoffs are associated with incredible optimism. Fear and greed. When the market falls, people think, "I'm going to lose all my money. Mother told me never to invest in stocks and she was right."

Brouwer: When is the best time to buy into a stock mutual fund?

Lynch: When the news is terrible. Remember back in 1981–1982 when we had a 20 percent prime rate, 12–13 percent unemployment, 15 percent inflation? People were talking about the world collapsing. That was the *greatest* time to buy stocks in the last 20 years.

Brouwer: The problem is most people think the reverse—that hard times are the worst time to invest.

Lynch: That's right. During a sharp downturn in the market, the newspapers and television reports sound terrible.

That doesn't tend to make people say, "Gee honey, let's put our life savings in the stock market." It's not the nature of people. In 1986–87 when the stock market was roaring along, corporate profits were good, that's when people said to themselves, "Now is the time to get in on the action."

Brouwer: They got in just in time for the crash in October, 1987.

Lynch: Right.

Brouwer: What are some rules of thumb for investing in a volatile market such as we have today?

Lynch: I would tell investors you have to ask yourself, "What am I going to do if this mutual fund goes down 30 percent or the market drops 500 points?" If the answer is, "I'm going to continue investing $1,000 or $5,000 or $50,000 a year," then that's fine. That person will eventually do extremely well, provided they picked solid mutual funds.

Brouwer: How can ordinary investors, people who have jobs and families, keep their emotions on a more even keel?

Lynch: You really have to detach yourself from the money you've invested. Obviously, you shouldn't invest money unless you've taken care of the basics—you have enough money to live on comfortably. When your stock mutual fund goes down, you have to say, "In this fund, I'm invested in McDonald's and they aren't going out of business, they're growing. And Ford and Merck, they're growing too." And so on.

Brouwer: And the stock market does come back. If you're patient for a year or so, things will turn around.

Lynch: We've had eight different times Magellan went down anywhere from 10 to 35 percent. Eight times. When the market goes down, Magellan is going to drop. I repeatedly tell people this. It's normal. Despite those eight significant downturns, the fund is up 12 times over the past 10 years.

Brouwer: With Magellan Fund you don't try to time the markets by moving in and out of stocks. This obviously works for you. Yet why is the public so fascinated with market timing and its many adherents and gurus?

Lynch: We've been on the planet maybe 5 million years or so and human nature hasn't changed all that much. It's that old battle between fear and greed.

Brouwer: I have never seen the classic market timing approach—charts, graphs, moving averages—work over the long haul.

Lynch: I'm in agreement there.

Brouwer: Obviously, Magellan is not in the category of the funds that try to profit from short-term market movements. What do you think is a good category or label for Magellan?

Lynch: Labels often do a disservice because the shareholder may think a growth fund will buy only high-growth stocks. With Magellan, I don't have a lot of prejudices. I bought General Public Utilities after they had the trouble with the Three Mile Island nuclear power plant they own. I bought Ford several years ago as a turnaround situation. It has been a capital appreciation fund.

Brouwer: No argument there. Though many people call it a growth fund, you wouldn't?

Lynch: I do not consider it a growth fund, where I buy only growth stocks. I try to participate in many types of companies. Even when the fund was small, I looked at all types—electric utilities, textile companies, big, little. I've always tried to look at all areas. That hasn't changed. I've always owned some conservative companies like Bristol-Myers. I've always owned some turnaround situations, cyclical stocks, growth stocks. I've tried to stay open to all ideas and all types of stocks in all fields. There is value everywhere.

Brouwer: Your point is that you have to have an open mind for value wherever you find it. And when things look bleak, when Wall Street doesn't want anything to do with an area—that's when you move?

Lynch: That's exactly my point. I'm willing to buy stocks when people consider them to be marginal. Many people wouldn't have bought casino companies because they think the Mafia runs them. I put 15 percent of my fund in that group at a time when many people wouldn't look at it. I'll buy anything if I think it has value. I've bought bankrupt companies. I think people are too narrow-minded. Too inflexible.

Brouwer: What factors have helped you be more broad-minded?

Lynch: I think it is being at Fidelity. We don't have a lot of rules. We don't have any economists. We don't have any people predicting the market. They just say, "Go out and make some money for your shareholders." I don't have to clear my selections with a bureaucratic structure. Plus, Magellan is a wide open fund. We aren't restricted to keeping a fixed percentage in bonds or cash. If you have a fund that has to deliver income, then you can't buy Chrysler at $5.

Brouwer: What about some of the other people at Fidelity? Do you benefit from sharing ideas with other portfolio managers?

Lynch: Yes. With 20 portfolio managers out looking for good stocks, I hear about lots of interesting situations. We have formal meetings once a month and ad hoc meetings during the day. We go around the room and tell about our three or four or five favorite stocks. And at the meetings, it is not a session where people rip up your ideas. The most we would say is, "It sounds pretty good, but I still prefer Manville or whatever."

I've seen organizations where people go in with a stock they like and they sort of crawl out of the room. We never do that. It sounds corny, but our meetings are 99 percent light and only one percent heat. I think in many situations I've seen, the numbers are reversed.

Brouwer: How important then is the fund's portfolio manager to overall success?

Lynch: The portfolio manager of a mutual fund is like a general who sets and directs strategy. It is not just the research staff. We have great analysts, but then so do many mutual fund groups. It is really the fund's portfolio manager that has to make the decision to buy or sell. If the general tells the troops to do something stupid, you've got lots of problems.

Brouwer: Since we're talking about management, when you analyze a stock, how much emphasis do you put on the quality of the company's management?

Lynch: Wall Street has always attached a lot of weight to a company's management. And if earnings went up, they assumed that had to do with management when, in fact, conditions may have been so good any fool could have done well in that business. Management is an important variable, but it's very hard to measure. So I usually bypass it and look directly at the nature of the business itself. Is it a good business? What is happening that might make it better? Or worse? I prefer to deal in facts rather than opinions.

Brouwer: What is a good business?

Lynch: I'd rather invest in a business that is so good that any fool could run it. Because eventually one will. Take technology for example. You have a business where you have to invent a new product every nine months. You have to anticipate what people will want and build a plant, set up distribution. Eventually, even the best managers will get their head handed to them in a business like that.

Brouwer: Okay, that's a bad business, what's a good one?

Lynch: Take someone who owns the only daily newspaper in a city. If one company doesn't want to advertise, another will. Higher demand for ads, just print a bigger paper. All you have to do is raise rates a little each year. Or take a gravel quarry in the Chicago area. Assume there are few competing quarries. All you have to do is keep your prices just under what it would cost for your competition to ship into your area. What a simple, wonderful business. You don't have to worry about Korean or Japanese imports or some guy from the Massachusetts Institute of Technology inventing a new rock.

Brouwer: Once you've bought a stock and it turns out badly, how do you eliminate ego from your decision-making process?

Lynch: You deal in facts. The facts are the stock you bought at $10 is now at $8. Things are not cooking. Perhaps there's a problem and the competition is intensifying. Maybe a new product isn't working. The stubborn person would just wait and hope things get better or even buy more. That's how you get in deep trouble. The reality is you make a lot of mistakes in this business. As long as you acknowledge your mistakes, you won't add to them. I've bought stocks at $10 that went to $14 and later to 25 cents. I've bought stocks that went from $10 to $4 and later to $40.

What I'm saying is that as long as the company is doing well . . . as long as I am happy with the company's financial position, I very well might buy more if the stock goes down.

Brouwer: How do you know the difference between the time to sell and the time to buy more?

Lynch: It is just self-confidence. If you don't understand what you own, you may get the perfect buying opportunity, but you won't take advantage of it. Rules don't always hold true. You have to use judgment. Even though the stock is down, you reassess your analytical work and if it still looks good, you may even buy more.

Brouwer: What is your personal benchmark for measuring Magellan's performance?

Lynch: Well it is all relative to the stock market. If my fund, or any similar fund, can't match or beat the market, then investors should go with something that can do better. That's really the fairest yardstick.

Brouwer: Why do so many stock mutual funds underperform the market averages?

Lynch: I don't know. This is something like the seventh straight year that the average mutual fund has under-performed the market. It is unprecedented in 50 years. I don't know why so many are doing badly.

Of course, there are many funds that are restricted to a certain type of stock—say growth stocks. But even there you have tremendous disparities.

Brouwer: Magellan is seldom number one in any given three-month period, yet it is always at or close to the top for longer periods. How does that work?

Lynch: It's a disservice to the public to focus on what's the best fund over the last three months, because very often investors will pile into that thing. If you have a small mutual fund that has a few hot stocks, that could give them great results for an entire year—up, say, 50 percent. But for someone putting $10,000 in the fund, they may be disappointed because next year the fund could conceivably go down 50 percent. One group of mutual funds is always going to be hot. Generally, these are nondiversified funds—mutual funds that can put 100 percent of their assets in gold or chemical stocks, whatever. Some portfolio manager with a few million in assets will buy Home Shopping Network and two or three other hot stocks and they'll be number one.

Brouwer: What is your performance goal relative to other mutual funds?

Lynch: My goal is to be in the top ten percent.

Brouwer: How have you done in view of that?

Lynch: 1989 was the 11th year out of 13 that Magellan has finished in the top ten percent of all funds.

Brouwer: Can you happily continue to run Magellan for another 10 or 20 years?

Lynch: Who knows? Maybe one day my wife gives me the call and says, "You've had it," then I'll leave [laughter]. Actually, I just take it day by day.

Brouwer: Does Fidelity have a contingency plan? Is there an heir apparent?

Lynch: You'll have to talk to somebody else at Fidelity about that. Fidelity is literally like the New York Yankees in the 1920s or the Boston Celtics in the 1960s. We have 20 portfolio managers who are outstanding. And there are another 20 or so who are good analysts. Maybe of that 20, another five or ten will be great portfolio managers. They're all around me. I guess that's the answer.

Brouwer: It is and it isn't. I am not just talking about someone being good; it is also a public awareness. Because investors identify you with Magellan, I think there would be a big outflow of assets if you retired.

Lynch: I wouldn't want to speculate on that issue, except to say I'm confident Magellan would continue to do well without me. Not a pleasant subject to discuss.

Brouwer: But it is critical. To your one million shareholders, this is certainly an issue of importance. Perhaps if Fidelity had someone working by your side...?

Lynch: But that's not the right person. The right person is someone off running another of our mutual funds—an outstanding moneymaker. And I suppose if I get hit by a truck, Fidelity would say, "Okay, now you're going to run Magellan." We have people like Morris Smith, Alan Leifer, George Vanderheiden, Beth Terrana, Rich Fenton. They are managing funds and making the tough decisions every day.

Brouwer: From a public relations viewpoint, I wonder if Fidelity has a plan to reassure investors that everything is being taken care of should you retire?

Lynch: Well, if they do have such a plan, they haven't bounced it off me.

Brouwer: Going beyond the mutual fund area, do you have a position on index arbitrage and some of the controversial Wall Street trading techniques these days?

Lynch: Well, I certainly think they should tighten up the margin requirements on options and futures trading. That's a definite. But it's more than that. When I first started in the investment business, people would speculate by buying shares in a small company. They would actually buy the shares. Now they buy an option on whether the overall market goes up or down. I mean, they might as well bet on whether it is going to rain in St. Louis next week.

Brouwer: The stock market is supposed to help make capital available to build our economy.

Lynch: That's right. But this kind of speculating does nothing for capital formation. And on a broader basis, the fact that the market goes up or down 190 points in a day discourages investors. They think it's like a lottery. They don't understand that to me and other portfolio managers (and ultimately, to the shareholders), what counts is what happens to the companies we invest in. This concern has gotten lost, and it's a discouraging environment.

Brouwer: Do you think that when an investor walks in the door at Pru-Bache or Shearson Lehman Hutton, they are likely to get good advice?

Lynch: They'll get the best advice the brokers have. But 20 or 30 years ago, the person they were assigned to would have been far more experienced.

Brouwer: Do you buy mutual funds for yourself and your family? And if so, do you buy any non-Fidelity funds?

Lynch: Sure I buy mutual funds. Just Fidelity. We've got enough great ones here.

Brouwer: What five or six Fidelity funds do you like?

Lynch: I like Fidelity Disciplined Equities and Fidelity Growth & Income. Growth & Income is a more conservative fund. It buys out-of-favor companies with high dividend yields, and it doesn't get hit too badly when the market drops. Fidelity Capital Appreciation, Fidelity OTC, Fidelity Growth, and Fidelity Special Situations.

Brouwer: And, of course, Magellan.

Lynch: Of course; didn't I mention that?

Brouwer: Who are some non-Fidelity portfolio managers you admire?

Lynch: John Neff (Windsor Fund), Mario Gabelli (Gabelli Asset Fund), Michael Price (Mutual Series Fund) and Richard Strong and William Corneliuson (Strong Total Return, Strong Investment), Matthew Weatherbie (Putnam Voyager), and Chuck Royce (Pennsylvania Mutual Fund).

Brouwer: Moving on, what gets you going in the morning? Money isn't an issue; you're financially secure. Famous. What's your motivation?

Lynch: No question, this business is fun for me. I have freedom to look at whatever companies and stocks I want. I travel, get out to see them. Plus, Fidelity is a great firm and a friendly one. We have free coffee and it's amazingly good. We have birthday parties for people. It's an exciting place, very stimulating. This is where I want to be.

And this is where Fidelity Magellan's 1 million shareholders want him to be. Poring over annual reports and visiting companies. Selling off the over-the-hill stocks and bringing in future star performers.

Mario Gabelli [see page 178] said to me, "Peter Lynch has one of the best jobs in the business. He gets to spend all of his day analyzing stocks with very little administrative stuff to distract him."

Perhaps that's why Lynch has been so successful. The folks at Fidelity had the sense to let him concentrate on what he does best—managing a portfolio of stocks.

One important aspect of his success has come from taking a stand at odds with the "accepted wisdom" on Wall Street. He trusts his instincts and his analysis when he takes very large positions in out-of-favor industries—insurance, autos, financial services.

And that's an important point. It's your money, so break free from the herd and think for yourself. As you become more informed, have faith in your own judgment. The tools are here. But you still have to have the courage to use them when your friends and relatives are going the opposite way.

7

Step by Step with Mutual Funds, from Buying In to Selling Out

On April 12, 1981, the United States' first space shuttle, Columbia, rocketed off its launch pad at Cape Kennedy. That much applied power was like lifting a skyscraper off its foundations and hurtling it into space. The enormous thrust was supplied by two solid fuel rocket boosters and one extended tank holding separate chambers of liquid oxygen and liquid hydrogen—a volatile and explosive combination when mixed together. At the end of the countdown, a pushed button climaxed years of preparation with a controlled explosion lifting man and metal off the gravity-bound earth, literally blasting through the atmosphere.

When watching such a dramatic event, we tend to focus on the critical steps of ignition and liftoff, yet those dramatic moments are only possible because of millions of hours of intense physical and mental preparation.

Your journey to financial success with no-load mutual funds certainly won't be as thrilling as a shuttle launch, but a successful liftoff is possible if you prepare properly. Then one day, the time for preparation is over, and the time comes to push the button and start investing.

Getting started requires faith in yourself and in the skills you've developed. You will be putting your money on the line. And instead of relying on advice from a friend or the latest investing "guru," you will be acting on your own hard-earned knowledge. For some that may be scary. Many people find it easier, more comforting, to put their money on the line when someone else is telling them what to do. But you won't need that crutch any more, because after having done your research, you know more than most investors.

When you put your money in a mutual fund, everything changes. No longer are these cold facts and figures. The names of the mutual funds you've chosen now hold your faith and your cash, and you worry. The research you've done may seem incomplete. You feel inadequate—wish you knew more. Don't panic. Every investment pro feels or has felt the same way. We always wish we knew more, had more time. But with investments, as in life, we can never know the future. Nor can we accurately predict how people and politicians— here and around the world—will react to future events. Life is uncertain; knowledge is inadequate, and facts and figures often unreliable.

In response to uncertainty, you can either wring your hands and stand by helplessly as events move past, or you can act. If you want investment success, you must start now. Action cures fear. Everything is ready—you've gone through and selected the mutual funds that suit you. Now is the time to push the button and get started.

BUYING IN: THE PAPER CHASE BEGINS

Buying into a fund means you will be inundated with paperwork. At first, it will be applications and prospectuses. When you send a check to the fund, you will receive confirmation slips, showing your purchase. By the way, when you send money to funds, use checks from an interest-bearing account if you have one. That way you earn interest until they cash your check.

Before long, you'll begin receiving statements from the fund as well. To keep you from drowning in a sea of paper, you need a way of recognizing and dealing with the important papers, while ignoring the rest.

Let's see what it really takes, step by step, to buy, track, and eventually sell a no-load mutual fund. No-load mutual fund shares are traditionally bought through the mail. First, the mutual fund sends you a prospectus. An application is enclosed separately or is part of the prospectus. There are two basic types of applications: one type for individuals, couples, and ordinary tax-paying investors, and a special type for Individual Retirement Accounts, corporate and unincorporated retirement plans, trusts, and other specialized accounts.

Make sure you fill out the right type of application. Though they are a bit confusing at first glance, if you follow the instructions carefully, you'll be okay. On Individual Retirement Account statements, the beneficiary section is very important. In effect, you are selecting someone to get the proceeds of your IRA account if you die. This is a requirement, so make sure you fill it out. If you neglect to fill in an important piece of information, the fund will probably send the application and your check back. Delays can keep your check in the U.S. mail system for several weeks, so be careful.

IT'S YOUR MONEY, SO PLAY IT SAFE

When you make an investment, keep a photocopy of the check and the application. These seldom get lost, but it does happen occasionally. At one time we dealt with mutual funds through the mails for all of our clients, and we did experience some problems.

Mutual Series Fund once booked a $100,000 check belonging to one of our clients into someone else's account. When we called, the fund had no record of our client's investment and, as they say on "Mission Impossible," they disavowed all knowledge of our client. After talking with a few clerks we got nowhere, so I asked Mike Price's assistant for help. (Mike is the president of Mutual Series Fund. You'll meet him in Chapter 10.) The check was found very quickly.

In the long run, it would have been discovered anyway, but who wants the aggravation and the grief of wondering where his or her money is tonight? To play it safe, keep proof of the date of your investment by sending your check via certified mail. An alternative would be to wire the money through a bank or use a discount broker.

Once the mutual fund receives your check, they will send a statement showing the date of purchase, amount purchased, the number of shares purchased and the price per share. Keep this; it is an important record.

SELLING OUT: HOW LONG CAN IT TAKE?

No matter how much you like a particular fund, the day will come when you sell part or all of your shares. There are four ways to go:

Telephone redemption: Some funds allow telephone redemptions, but if you want this privilege, you have to check the appropriate box on the application when you buy in.

Liquidating letter: Most funds require a letter from you before they will sell, and your signature has to be guaranteed by a bank or brokerage firm.

Sale through a brokerage firm: If you bought your shares through a brokerage, you can sell shares simply by giving them a call. If you bought shares directly from a mutual fund and have decided to use a broker. you can sign what is called a stock power. This is an instruction from you to the mutual fund, telling the fund to transfer your shares to the brokerage account. Once that is accomplished, you can sell the shares any time you want.

By writing a check: Many mutual funds, primarily money market funds, allow you to write checks against the assets in your account. Since money market funds have a constant one dollar per share price, this is easy to track. But some funds are offering check-writing privileges against bond funds, in particular Treasury bond and Ginnie Mae funds. This practice poses special investment and record-keeping problems. We'll cover this in more detail later in this chapter, in the section, "Keeping It Straight."

When you sell out, the check will come to you at the address on the application. Make sure you notify the fund if your address changes. Generally, this has to be done in a letter from you, and your signature must be guaranteed by a bank or brokerage firm. All checks will be made out to the person whose name is on the account. This is also the person who will incur taxable income. If you have an account with a friend or relative, the gains and losses are considered a joint responsibility, but are reported only for the social security number given on the application. Think carefully about how you are opening the account before you actually do it. Do it right the first time because the legal title or name on an account is difficult to alter once in the mutual fund management company's computer.

When you sell, it can take quite a while to get your money. If a fund located in Boston liquidates your account and sends you a check on Monday, you may not get the check until Saturday, when your bank is closed. Next, you hustle to the bank on Monday and deposit the check. Then you write a check to the next mutual fund you want to invest in.

You're smart, so when you write your check to the new fund, you use an interest-bearing account. But they're smart too. They cash the check on Friday, the day they get it, but because it arrived after 12 noon, their time, you get the next day's price. That's Monday. The fund earns interest on your money over the weekend. Your check was in the mail from your old fund for seven days, and you lost two days of interest going into the new one. Total: nine days of missed interest.

How do you calculate the lost interest for nine days? Simple. Take the annual rate for your money market fund or bank account, and multiply it by the amount of your investment. Then divide that amount by 365 days in the year.

$$\$10,000 \times .06(6\%) = \$600,$$
$$\$600/365 = \$1.64,$$
$$\$1.64 \times 9 = \$14.79 \text{ (lost interest for nine days).}$$

This equals the daily rate of interest you would have been earning in the money market fund or the bank, multiplied by the number of days the money was in the mail or otherwise unavailable to earn interest for you.

USING A DISCOUNT BROKER FOR MUTUAL FUND TRADES

Recently, discount stock brokerage firms have begun making things easier for mutual fund investors. You can now buy no-load mutual funds in a brokerage account just by picking up the phone. Charles Schwab & Company and its Mutual Fund Marketplace are the most well-known, but there are other firms who offer this service as well.

Two large discount brokers that let you buy and sell no-load mutual funds are:

Charles Schwab & Company
101 Montgomery Street
San Francisco, CA 94104
(800) 648-5300

Fidelity Investments
164 Northern Avenue
Boston, MA 02210
(800) 544-6666

Without a doubt, these firms make it easier to buy and sell no-load mutual funds. You simply have to decide if the convenience is worth the cost. For example, Schwab's current rate for a $10,000 purchase is $44 plus two-tenths of one percent. Two-tenths percent of $10,000 is $20. Added to the flat rate, that totals $64. You would be paying $64, or six-tenths of a percent, for convenience. When you sell, you would pay a similar rate. However, if you sell one fund and buy another with the proceeds that day, you pay a reduced commission ($10) on the shares purchased.

There are several advantages of working through a reputable brokerage firm:

☐ Consolidated statement showing all mutual fund positions. You don't have to reconcile statements from several mutual funds to see where you stand.

☐ Easier record keeping. Because everything is in one place and on one statement, it's easier to track your buys and sells, dividends, interest, and capital gains or losses at tax time.

☐ Your money spends more time working for you. If you invest in a fund through the mail, you have to send in a check and this may take a week. When you sell, the mutual fund sends you a check, so your money is out of the market and in the mail for as much as a week. With a brokerage account, the proceeds from a sale should be in your account earning interest the next business day after you sell a fund.

TRACKING YOUR FUNDS

Once you own mutual funds, how do you track them? Most investors simply look in the paper each day to check the price of their funds. This is a daily ritual many people enjoy, and that's fine, but don't delude yourself into thinking this means you are watching or tracking your funds. Prices reflect events after they happen. What you really need is an objective method of analyzing your funds to see if they compare favorably to other investments you could have chosen.

WATCH YOUR FUNDS LIKE A HUNGRY HAWK

You need to train yourself to watch your funds like a hawk. A hawk shows mild interest when things are normal and not much is going on. But when something important, like food, shows up, the fierce-looking bird focuses intently and swoops down.

Here's a simple three-step method to track funds you own:

- ☐ Read the quarterly report (some funds only provide a semiannual report). This may sound simplistic, but many investors don't.
- ☐ Check the quarterly performance (total return); compare it to the appropriate index (S & P 500, Salomon Brothers Corporate Bond, or Shearson Lehman Intermediate Government Bond Index.
- ☐ Compare the portfolio listed in this quarterly report with the last one.

What should you learn from this? First, the president or chairman will talk about investment performance and their outlook for the future. Look for a consistent management philosophy from quarter to quarter. Second, by comparing the quarterly performance with an index, you get a solid benchmark to see how well your fund did. For example, a good growth and income mutual fund should perform much better than the S & P 500 in a down market, and should stay fairly close to the stock index in an up market. On the other hand, a good growth fund will probably go down about as much as the S & P 500 in a down market, and it should beat the index in an up market.

If your fund does well compared to its appropriate index, then you're in good shape. Finally, a look at the portfolio this quarter will also tell you, at a glance, how optimistic the portfolio manager is, and will also flag any changes in investment philosophy. Look at the portfolio to see what percent is in stocks, bonds, and cash equivalents. Has this changed from last quarter?

The percentage of cash equivalents in the fund isn't entirely under the control of the portfolio manager because there may be many new investors coming in, or old investors selling out. Nonetheless, this mix is very important to the overall success of the fund, so look at it. Also, look at the percentage of stocks in any one industry group, and, as much as you can, look to see if the fund is buying different types of stocks: OTC versus Fortune 500. If there are bonds in the portfolio, look at the maturity to see if it has changed on average.

This may sound like a lot of work, but it won't take you more than an hour or so each quarter. Isn't 60 minutes every few months a reasonable amount of time to spend watching your money—instead of television?

DON'T FORGET YOUR OLD FRIEND *WIESENBERGER*

Once a quarter you can also make a trip back to the public library. Ask for the *Wiesenberger* quarterly updates or the *Barron's* issue that contains Mike Lipper's quarterly performance data. In either of these sources, you can see the quarterly returns for your mutual funds, as well as any other funds you are interested in. In addition, you can check any of the magazines (*Forbes, Money, Business Week*, and *Changing Times*) that print mutual fund comparisons. See what they think of your funds. You may also hear of a fund that's worth looking into.

You may also find a mutual fund newsletter that you like. There are many of them, some with excellent track records. If you see one that looks interesting, call or write and ask for a sample copy. Most newsletters have low-cost introductory offers or you may be able to find them at your public library. If you do use a newsletter, remember that they often pay too much attention to short-term investment performance. If you get too caught up in monthly or quarterly comparisons, it will drive you crazy. Even the greatest funds do not pump out steady quarterly returns. There are times when they beat the market and times when the market outpaces them. Don't put too much emphasis on quarterly results. You should look at them, but don't get an itchy trigger finger.

Whatever sources of information you use, your strategy should be to find and use mutual funds with solid, proven investment techniques. At times, a particular investment style will be out of favor, and funds that use it will lag the market. But remember, both top mutual funds and Super Bowl winners find it hard to repeat. This year's poorer performers may be next year's top ones.

KEEP IT STRAIGHT (RECORDKEEPING AND TAXES)

Some of the following suggestions come from my own experience and many come from two pros on mutual fund taxation, John Foppiano and Robert Sherwood. Both are certified public accountants with Price Waterhouse, the "Big Six" accounting firm, in its Boston office. Price Waterhouse handles many of the largest mutual fund families—Putnam, Colonial, Loomis-Sayles, Fidelity, American Capital, T. Rowe Price, Vanguard, and many more. Foppiano, a partner in the office, has 30 years experience with mutual funds. Sherwood, a partner, has been specializing in mutual fund taxation for 11 years.

The tax information accompanying your year-end mutual fund statement may have been written with the help of one of these gentlemen. Their job is advising mutual funds managers on how to explain the new tax changes to their clients. Though many funds do a reasonably good job of explaining things, you have to keep up your end, which is recordkeeping.

DO IT RIGHT THE FIRST TIME

The best advice is to start right and keep solid records. Mutual fund computers generate a statement whenever there is activity in the account, such as dividends being paid or shares being bought or sold. Mutual funds pay out dividends and interest quarterly or monthly. Capital gains are generally paid out once or twice a year. To make sure you have not missed anything, keep everything you get from the mutual fund during the year. Some funds provide a summary of the year's activity; some don't. After January 1, you can go through what you have and throw out any duplicative statements. But you must keep your essential records for at least three years from the date you file your tax return; essential records include any income earned from the fund and/or gains or losses from the sale of fund shares.

Keep your records for each fund in one file. If you sell shares in a fund, make a photocopy of the statement that shows the trade and put that with your tax records. That way, if you are questioned by the Internal Revenue Service for that year, you have the backup documentation and you don't have to hunt around for it.

We all know *what* we should be doing; the hardest thing is to actually *do it*. Make it easy on yourself. Set up the file as soon as you make the investment. When statements and reports come in, put them in the file immediately. That way, you know you have the information.

TAX BASIS AND OTHER STUPEFYING TOPICS

Okay, let's be honest—you're dying of boredom. Believe me, I'm with you. Not even John Foppiano and Bob Sherwood from Price Waterhouse get excited reading about taxes. But you have to do it. Keep plugging along; you'll make it.

The biggest record-keeping problem you will have is figuring out your tax basis or cost of shares when you sell. For example, when a fund declares a dividend, that is a taxable event for you, whether they send you a check or reinvest the dividends in more shares of the fund. When it comes time to sell, you don't want to pay taxes again. Once is bad enough. So you must calculate the adjusted cost or basis of your shares.

LIGHT READING: IRS PUBLICATION 564

Rather than getting bogged down in the fine points of mutual fund taxation, I will simply suggest you get a copy of Internal Revenue Service Publication 564, entitled *Mutual Fund Distributions*. This publication covers all the bases on mutual fund taxation. It includes

☐ A Mutual Fund Record chart.
☐ A sample 1099 form.
☐ A sample 1040 U.S. Individual Income Tax Return.
☐ Schedule B—Interest and Dividend Income.

This publication is available free from any local Internal Revenue Service office.

In January of each year, the mutual fund will send you a 1099 form listing dividends, interest, capital gains distributions, investment expenses, and nontaxable distributions, if there are any. Those who hold shares at a brokerage firm will be receiving this information directly from the firm, rather than from each of the mutual funds. This is the information you or your accountant will need to prepare your tax return. Start your mutual fund files right away. Maintain them carefully and you will be glad you did.

TELEPHONE SWITCH INVESTORS DO IT MORE OFTEN

That's right; if you do a lot of buying and selling, or telephone switch speculating, I hope you like bookkeeping and paying taxes. Some fund families offer shareholders the right to switch from one fund in the group to another just by making a call. As usual, some people use this feature to move like jackrabbits from one fund to another. If you are a telephone switch speculator and you don't like bookkeeping, you're in for a nightmare. You will have a large number of transactions to account for; each time you switch, you are selling one fund and buying another. The fund will be reporting each sale to the Internal Revenue Service on a 1099-B form. This form notifies Uncle Sam that you sold some shares and may owe taxes on that amount.

Frankly, if you try market timing or telephone switching, I think you will find the investment results are not worth it. Even if you want to try, the tax recordkeeping requirements are so daunting that you may decide to do it only in a tax-deferred account such as an Individual Retirement Account.

THE BOOMERANG

Investors who own shares in corporate bond and government securities funds sometimes receive a return of their original capital. In effect, they send the money off to the fund and start getting it back a few months later. I call this the boomerang effect. This occurs whenever the fund pays out more than it makes in a year's time.

For example, if a mutual fund decided to pay a 10 percent yield, but the fund's net investment return after expenses was 9 percent, then the balance they pay out is your own money coming back. It's called return of capital. Why invest your money in a fund, only to have them send it back? It sounds silly, but that is exactly what dozens of mutual funds are doing.

To avoid return of capital, stay away from bond funds paying higher than market yields. If Treasury bonds are yielding 10 percent, then a fund can only pay you a net of about 9.25 percent after fund expenses. If they are paying more than that, it may very well be a return of capital. This is a poor investment practice, because you are getting your capital back and it's out of action until you reinvest. Plus, some investors don't realize they're getting a return of capital and they spend it, thinking they got a high return. Thus, their principal is shrinking.

Also, return of capital makes for very messy bookkeeping. When you have a return of capital, you have to reduce the cost of the shares you still own. Later on, when you sell, this catches up to you in the form of higher taxes.

Since many bond funds offer check-writing, you can inadvertently complicate your tax situation if you use this feature. Though you may not think of it as selling shares, that is exactly what happens if you write a check against a bond fund you own. Every time you write a check, the fund sells shares to raise cash to cover your check. With a bond fund this gives you a taxable event or sale. What a nightmare trying to track each sale (check). No matter how convenient it seems, do *not* write checks against anything but a money market fund. Check-writing works well with money market funds because their shares are always priced at one dollar per share, so there are no gains or losses to calculate.

KEEP IT SIMPLE

Keeping good records for taxes is very easy if you keep it simple. To start right and keep it straight, you should have a separate file for each mutual fund you own. In each file you need two subfiles: one for the prospectus, statement of additional information, quarterly, semiannual, and annual reports and other investment and general information; and the second, for quarterly and annual statements and other tax-related information, such as 1099 forms. The quarterly report is a statement of financial changes in the fund and of investment returns, and an analysis of the fund's investment outlook. The quarterly and annual statements show the value of your holdings, the amount of dividends and interest, and whether your dividends and interest were reinvested, all the interesting financial details you love to read about.

Set files up as soon as you decide to invest. The quarterly reports are critical, and they should be kept in your files so you can compare and contrast the last report with the current one. Statements, reports, and miscellaneous papers may turn your mailbox into a trashbin, but don't ignore them. This is the crucially important, yet unglamorous side of investing.

COUNTDOWN

When a space shuttle lifts off the pad, there are several astronauts on board. We know their names and consider them heroes, and they are. But there are thousands of others who strain and struggle every day. They turn screws and sew the airsuits. They run computer simulations and do safety tests. They make decisions and judgments that will have a huge impact on the success of the mission and the safety of the astronauts.

Tracking your funds and keeping good records are not glamorous, front-line chores, but they are important to a successful liftoff with mutual funds. Give some time and energy to the nuts and bolts of your investment vehicle. Do a good job of recordkeeping. One important tax tip is to keep track of purchase dates, particularly for large purchases. This may help you reduce taxes when you sell. One mistake to avoid is buying into a mutual fund just before it pays a large dividend. This usually occurs at year's end.

Track performance carefully each quarter. Don't let complacency and carelessness lead to serious problems. These simple precautions and routine maintenance procedures will keep your portfolio humming. And when you push the button at the end of the countdown, don't forget the more mundane yet critical steps needed to keep your investments firmly targeted on your goals.

8

Take the Time to Learn, or It May Cost You Money— Lots and Lots of Money

Looking back on those early days, I can't believe how naive I was. When Merrill Lynch hired me to go through the industry's "finest" training program, I thought I was part of Wall Street's A team. It was the proudest moment of my life—but not for long.

My motives for getting into the investment business were pretty simple. I liked investing and spent my free time studying and reading about ways to make money in the markets. I also wanted to work with people, not machines, and I was ready to tackle a business where my income depended solely on how hard and smart I worked.

So I fused my nose to the grindstone and quickly became one of the rising stars in the San Francisco office. A few years later, I moved from the ranks of the "baby" brokers sitting out in "the bullpen" to my own private corner office. And it was in that office, one day in the spring of 1983, that I realized I had to leave the firm.

What triggered my decision? One day our office manager, my "boss," came in and sat down. I had heard he was under a lot of pressure from higher-ups to increase the office's profitability by moving "product." Most people don't think of investments—stocks, bonds, and mutual funds—as "products." They don't realize that, even though they may be putting a good chunk of their life's savings or discretionary dollars into an investment, to most brokerage firms that investment is just a product that must be moved *off the shelf*. It's no different from a loaf of bread at a supermarket or a microwave oven at a department store.

My firm seemed to have this basic attitude towards brokers: If your "production" was strong, you were great, wonderful, and a credit to the firm and your family. If you were having an off month, you didn't exist. You were nobody. If you had a few off months in a row, you were chewing gum on the sole of a shoe. The bottom line was, "What have you done for the firm today?" Brokerage firm officers and executives are under intense pressure to pump up profits. Their careers may be on the line if profits don't come through, because Wall Street firms are notorious for rapid layoffs in bear markets.

I believe my boss was really driven by this pressure from above. Outside of the office he was a great guy. He and his wife were fun-loving people who threw wonderful parties. She was lovely, gracious, and intelligent; her own person, not just a tag-along executive wife. He was a good family man, well respected in the community—in his heart, a good person. Meet him socially, and you would have no idea of the pressure he could put on his brokers. But on the job, he really knew how to tighten the vise.

For instance, that day, he came into my office, sat down, and said, "I came in to ask you how much of the health sciences trust you're going to do." This was a new mutual fund Merrill was helping to sell. In my mind, there were two obvious problems with it. First, being new, it had no track record. Since there were many established mutual funds with good track records, why should I risk my clients' money and shoot craps with an unknown? It's like paying $100,000 to a sidewalk painter who tells you he's the next Picasso. Possible, but unlikely. I hate new offerings in general because they play on the latest fads—whatever is hot. They may tout an interesting but risky investment gimmick, but the fact that it is untried is buried in the fine print.

My second concern was that this particular fund invested in only one industry—it was a sector fund, probably the most aggressive type of mutual fund. Concentration in one industry puts the portfolio manager in a straitjacket. Even if the entire industry was performing sluggishly, the mutual fund manager had to put all of the investors' money into those stocks—on the line—anyway. I simply did not like the fund. It was too risky.

But, as our chieftains frequently told us, our job was to sell, not to be investment analysts. This is a crucial fact of life on Wall Street and on Main Street. Brokers are men and women who are paid solely when they sell you something that, hopefully, pays a juicy commission.

HOW MUCH PRODUCT WAS I GOING TO MOVE?

My boss thought my opinion on the fund's merits was unimportant. He demanded an answer: *How much product was I going to move?* This particular deal was like many others on the shelf at Merrill Lynch and other large brokerage firms. About once a month, the firm came up with a new offering that it really wanted to push. Why? Because the firm and its brokers pocketed more money on new offerings than on routine buy and sell transactions.

To top it off, one of the firm's marketing brains had decided to put a little show biz into the act. To promote the health sciences trust, my boss dressed up as a medical doctor and paraded around the office goading brokers to sell. That was somebody's idea of innovative marketing.

At 7:45 A.M. that day, my stomach was upset, and I was not in the mood to be put on the spot by an ersatz Marcus Welby.

The pressure built as I saw the "doctor" going around to other brokers with a white smock, a stethoscope, and one of those reflector headbands you see in mail order health insurance ads. I felt sorry for him, but I really didn't think it was a good investment for my clients. And after all, that's whom I was working for.

As soon as he sat down in my office, things got ugly fast. I don't remember if we screamed at each other or if we just snarled. We both were under a lot of pressure. I knew right then I had a choice to make. I could back off and shut up, but the scene would be replayed the next week or the next month. To stay with the firm, I had to play the game. In my mind, this would have been putting the firm's interests ahead of my customers'. I decided not to; so a few months later, I walked out the door.

THE COMMISSION SYSTEM: SAY GOODBYE TO OBJECTIVE ADVICE

I was still naive when I left Merrill Lynch. I thought the problem was simply confined to big brokerage firms with hundreds of offices and cadres of fast-track executives lusting for bonuses—people who didn't really care about clients. So I became a partner in the San Francisco office of Boettcher & Company, a regional investment banking company—a smaller, less structured, more people-oriented firm. It didn't help. The problem, I discovered, isn't size, and it isn't aggressive pressure-cooked bosses or sales managers. It's *the commission system*. Walk in the door at any brokerage firm, and you are likely to collide with the same problem. You think you're getting objective investment advice, but the person you talk to is simply a salesperson.

This isn't just my personal view. The laws that govern brokerage and investment firms make it clear that a broker's compensation is tied strictly to the act of buying and selling stocks or bonds or other investments. Any advice given is *incidental* to the normal task of executing transactions. It took me several years to make this connection—to realize how this one factor can influence the thinking of brokers, no matter how honorable their intentions.

In the last few years many brokerage firms have almost magically transformed their brokers into financial advisers or planners or consultants. These attempts at restoring dignity to the troops are little more than window dressing. Flashy brochures and a new title don't change people or the system, and they won't protect you and your money if you run into a commission-hungry salesperson.

There's nothing wrong with doing business with a salesperson. Selling is the engine that drives the economy. Much of the success of our economic system rests on the shoulders of hard-working salespeople. But when you need advice, you want it unbiased and objective. When your life's savings are on the line, you don't want to be shoved into the latest hot deal of the week.

This may sound cruel, but many brokers are little more than high-pressure salespeople. Ethics, professionalism, and integrity are words they spout glibly with no understanding. Their job is to "close," to influence you to buy something, anything with a fat commission. Closers are dangerous to your financial health and well-being. In order to prosper, you must avoid these peddlers who roam the financial horizon touting the latest investment fad or gimmick.

BUT DON'T JUST TAKE MY WORD FOR IT

Let's see what some of the country's top investment pros think about the quality of investment advice you're likely to get from brokerage firms. You've already met Charles Schwab and Peter Lynch, and in Chapter 10 you're going to meet several more top pros. I asked a few of them for their opinion on this subject.

Charles Schwab

Brouwer: What do you think of the type of advice someone is going to get walking in the door at a large brokerage firm?

Schwab: First, I think investors should weigh *all* advice very carefully, no matter what the source. But, in particular, advice from stockbrokers is very suspect in my opinion.

Brouwer: Why is that?

Schwab: Conflict of interest. I can't overstress the fact that brokers only make money—make commissions—when the investor buys or sells. The more transactions, the more they make. To get you to buy and sell more often, they play on your emotions—fear and greed.

Mario Gabelli

(Founder of The Gabelli Group, which manages five mutual funds—Gabelli Asset, Gabelli Growth, Gabelli Value, Gabelli Convertible, and Gabelli Equity Trust. In addition, his GAMCO Investors manages money for pension plans, endowments, and individual investors. Total assets under management are $6.5 billion.)

Brouwer: You have worked at several different brokerage firms before starting your own firm. Can people get good information and objective advice from the major brokerage firms?

Gabelli: Yes . . . maybe. The problem is that good brokers understand that their book of business depends entirely on the loyalty of their customers. Unfortunately, the young guys who dial for dollars are often on what Wall Street calls "a search and destroy mission." You search for customers and if you destroy them, you just search for new ones.

Brouwer: What do you think is a better system?

Gabelli: Brokers are subject to a lot of internal pressures. If he doesn't generate enough revenue, his chair is given to someone else. And so you have a problem.

Brouwer: As an alternative, do you think people can do well if they simply invest in a portfolio of quality no-load mutual funds? No in-and-out trading, just long-term buy and hold?

Gabelli: I think your approach to finding the highest quality no-loads makes a lot of sense. And it goes in the client's best interest. So you are at the cutting edge of where the Street should be. You know it and I know it.

Stephen Lieber

(Founder of the Evergreen Fund.)

Brouwer: What chance does someone walking in the door at a large brokerage firm have of getting decent investment advice?

Lieber: It's marginal. It depends on whose hands they fall into. If it is a good broker, fine. But there's a low probability you'll get really good service.

Brouwer: A lot of the firms are emphasizing high-commission investments—unit investment trusts, limited partnerships, load mutual funds. Is there any economic justification for that other than fatter earnings for them?

Lieber: No. It's just merchandise. The industry, which used to proclaim a certain professionalism, now is primarily a merchandising business.

Michael Price

(President of the Mutual Series Fund.)

Brouwer: Do you think someone walking in the door of a big brokerage firm has much of a chance to get good investment return?

Price: You know, it all depends on the guy you get to.

Brouwer: Normally the good brokers aren't going to be taking people walking in off the street.

Price: That's right. And there are very few good brokers. Most of the brokers sell the product that the brokerage firms develop. And I think those products are developed to make money for the broker rather than the client. So, the answer is no, people aren't likely to get good advice. The way to invest is to understand what you're doing. To understand what values are.

Claude Rosenberg, Jr.

(Founder of RCM Capital Management.)

Brouwer: What about people who go to a broker for advice?

Rosenberg: Let the buyer beware. There are good brokers, but you can't assume a firm's name means anything. Many financial planners and brokers are like salespeople in department stores—selling whatever's on the shelf. They have become mere product salesmen as opposed to advisers. I think that's the problem. And that's the challenge for the average investor. Can you find a broker who is really concentrating on what is best for you as opposed to what is best for him?

Jack Leylegian

(President of Leylegian Investment Management.)

Brouwer: I have no problem with someone using a broker, if the broker really does his or her job—analyzing, recommending, and being knowledgeable about mutual funds and other investments. But what is the likelihood of finding such a broker?

Leylegian: Very small. I think the average broker is not qualified to give good advice. Most people who go into a brokerage firm with a big name on the door assume they're going to get the best advice.

Brouwer: Why don't they?

Leylegian: Number one, a broker's background, education, and training are in marketing primarily, not investments.

Number two, the compensation system is all wrong. Most brokers sell you whatever gives the fattest commission. And if a broker doesn't do that, the firm lets him go.

You will get a chance to hear more from each of these and other investment pros in Chapter 10. As you can see, they are highly skeptical about your chances of getting objective advice from people who rely on commissions for a living. One of the biggest problems is that salespeople tend to take the path of least resistance. They find it easiest to sell whatever is hot. Who wouldn't? But the quick and easy way for them usually turns out to be the wrong way for you.

A QUICK STUDY OF LOAD VERSUS NO-LOAD OR WHY PAY A COMMISSION?

How can you stay out of the grasp of unscrupulous, ignorant, or unprofessional salespeople? It's simple: *Never invest in anything that pays a juicy commission.* By not using high-commission load mutual funds you avoid the possibility of running afoul of an unscrupulous salesperson. And since there is no statistical difference in performance between load and no-load mutual funds, why fork over your cash?

To prove the point, let's examine some funds with 10-year track records listed in the *Wiesenberger Investment Company Service* you used in Chapter 5. In the section called "Management Results: Total Return," look at the cumulative results for whatever period you want to study. I consulted a copy of *Wiesenberger* and chose funds with 10-year records listed under the heading "Maximum Capital Gains." There were 63 mutual funds in that category, of which 29 were no-loads and 34 were load funds. I checked in the "Mutual Funds Panorama" section to see which ones have sales charges or loads. The average performance for each category is shown on the following page. Remember, this study of performance did not include the sales charges on the load funds. Investors in load funds would have received less than the average shown, because

10-YEAR AVERAGE CUMULATIVE PERFORMANCE

Load mutual funds	+ 396.0 percent[1]
No-load mutual funds	+ 435.1 percent

[1]Net results to investors would be lower due to sales charges.

they had to pay a commission that came off the top before their dollars were invested.

Sixty-three funds is not a large sample, but I wasn't trying to be exhaustive. I just want to show you how it's done. I compared total return of load funds versus no-loads by averaging the cumulative performance.

Next, I picked the top 10 performers without regard to whether they were load or no-load, to see if the ratio of no-load funds in the top 10 equaled the ratio of no-loads overall. There were seven no-load mutual funds in the top 10. As no-load funds represent 46 percent of the group as a whole, this showing in the top 10 was very good.

Very often when I'm speaking at a seminar, someone asks me how no-load funds make money. How can they pay their bills if they don't charge a load or commission? The questioner doesn't understand that very little of the load or commission goes to the mutual fund itself. Mostly it goes to a network of brokers or financial planners who are selling the fund. In other words, load funds use the money to pay for a distribution system. All funds, both load and no-load, rely on the 0.5 to 1 percent investment management fee to pay their bills and turn a profit.

Some families of mutual funds that used to be no-load are now adding sales charges to build their empires and run huge advertisements for their current "hot" fund. Since you want to build your wealth, not somebody's empire, stick to no-load mutual funds. And whenever you hear a too-good-to-be-true sales pitch, you can be certain of two things: it *is* too good to be true, and it probably pays someone a big commission. Just smile and walk away, secure in the knowledge that you are on track to build *your* wealth and financial security, not theirs.

9

Retirement: If You Fail to Plan, You're Planning for Failure

Hour after hour, year after year—time trudges on.   In most human endeavors, time weakens and erodes. Yet with investments, time builds wealth and can rebuild weakened resources. The magic of compound interest can turn solid, growing investments into a future fortune. Ask yourself, am I letting time be my ally or my enemy?

Why do we waste our most valuable investment resource— time: Is it ignorance? Impatience? A concern only for today? These are the human weaknesses that can, in later years, produce poverty and a degrading dependence on social security or charity.

SAVE AND INVEST NOW OR SCRIMP LATER

How many retired people do you know who are forced to scrimp to survive? Some are simply the victims of misfortune, but many are not. Before they retired, many people worked hard, but they neglected to sow the seeds of future prosperity. And that's too bad, because preparing for the future is not that difficult. A single dollar saved and invested 50 years ago would have grown, at 10 percent per year, to $117 today.

Many older people think back to the days of the Great Depression when steak was a few cents a pound and milk just pennies a half gallon. They miss the point. Steak and milk have to be consumed, but a share of stock or a piece of real estate would be here today. Thinking back, they should bemoan the neglected opportunity to put cash into common stocks or real estate that then sold for a fraction of its value today. Poverty was widespread in the 1930s; many people had no money to spare. But what's the excuse for the 1950s, 1960s, or 1970s? Each of us, myself included, has missed opportunities simply because we failed to focus on the future.

Those opportunities are long gone, but yours are here now. Don't pass up shares in a mutual fund for the thrill of a new Toyota or the immediate satisfaction of a steak grilling on a new backyard deck and built-in barbecue. Save and invest now; spend and enjoy later.

COMPOUND INTEREST CAN AND SHOULD WORK FOR YOU

This isn't a plea for self-sacrifice, it's a reminder to think about your own self-interest. Look out for number one as you take a minute to think about these numbers. One thousand dollars invested today at a steady 10 percent will be worth an astounding $45,259.26 in 40 years. But that same investment only builds to $17,449.40 in 30 years, and the total drops to $6,727.50 for a 20-year period. The difference is simply the buildup of interest earning interest over many years. So the effort to save and invest very modest amounts in your early years will repay itself many times over.

You probably are saying, "Forty years? Who cares? I won't be around then." You're wrong. A healthy 30-year-old person has an average life expectancy of 52.2 years. And our life expectancy is increasing, thanks to better diets and scientific advancements. Also, even if you're not around, someone you love will be. Your husband or wife, your children, grandchildren, brothers, sisters. A charity or a cause you believe in. And just because you invest now, nothing says you must wait 40 years to spend your profits. By starting now you increase your earning power, your personal leverage. The earlier you start, the more potent your dollars are, thanks in large part to the magic of compound interest.

Inertia isn't your only obstacle to a comfortable retirement. Taxes can also sap the strength of strategies striving for financial independence. You get a handsome payoff from an investment, and then the Internal Revenue Service takes a big bite out. That slows down the compounding effect. Look at the same 10 percent compounded return growing over 40 years, first for a tax-deferred investment, and then for an investment taxable in a 35 percent bracket (combined state and federal tax).

Tax-deferred investment growth:

$$\$10,000 \ @10\% \text{ for 40 years } = \$452,592.56.$$

Taxable investment growth:

$$\$10,000 \ @6.5\% \ (10\% - 3.5\% \text{ taxes) for 40 years}$$

$$= \$124,160.75.$$

Common sense tells us the tax-deferred return of 10 percent will grow faster than a net after-tax return of 6.5 percent, but as you can see the tax-deferred account is fatter by over three and a half times. What happened? Money that would ultimately go to pay taxes earned dividends and interest in the meantime. True, the tax-deferred account will eventually be cut back by taxes, but the net result will still be much larger.

There are a number of ways to earn tax-free or tax-deferred income. Tax-free municipal bond funds pay interest free from federal income taxes, and very often state income taxes as well. (See Chapter 4 for examples.)

TAX-DEFERRED RETIREMENT PLANS: PAINLESS, POTENT

The best way to defer taxes is through a retirement plan. They come in many forms today; the most common are Individual Retirement Accounts (IRAs), self-employed retirement plans (Keogh or H.R. 10 plans), and corporate or government retirement plans. Most working people qualify for one or more of these plans. And they generally offer two immense advantages. First, the money you contribute is usually not taxed before you put it in. Second, the interest, dividends, and capital appreciation you earn are not taxed until you take the money out.

The best known type of retirement plan is the Individual Retirement Account. If you earn a salary or wages, you can contribute as much as 100 percent of your salary or wages up to a maximum of $2,000. If you are married, and your spouse has no salary or wage income, you may increase that to $2,250. If you or your spouse are *not* covered under another type of retirement plan, you may deduct your contribution from your taxable income.

If you or your spouse are covered under another retirement plan, to take the full deduction you must have an adjusted gross income of no more than $25,000 (single) or $40,000 (married, filing jointly). The deduction is gradually phased out as the adjusted gross income goes from $25,000 to $35,000 (single) or from $40,000 to $50,000 (married, filing jointly).

JANUARY 2 OR APRIL 15?

Procrastination is the arch-enemy of the Individual Retirement Account; make your annual contributions as early as you can. There's no need to wait to contribute to your IRA until next year on April 15; you can fund it each year on January 2. That gives you more than a year of additional tax-deferred growth. Or if you can't contribute $2,000 all at once, put in your cash as you accumulate it throughout the year until you reach the maximum.

IS AN IRA STILL WORTHWHILE? YOU BET IT IS

Now that the deductibility of IRA contributions has been reduced, many people are less likely to set one up. Those who have one may not contribute. This is because they believe the chief benefit is the tax deduction. But though this is an immediate and obvious benefit, it's far from the most important. The biggest benefit is long-term, tax-deferred growth for your later years. Even if you cannot deduct your contribution, you should still contribute the maximum. A deduction is nice, but long-term compounding is remarkable. Albert Einstein himself once said, "The most amazing mathematical phenomenon is the magic of compounded interest." Here's why:

If you, starting at age 30, put $2,000 in an Individual Retirement Account every year until age 70, you will have contributed $80,000. At 10 percent a year, your account would be worth approximately $975,000! Even if you pay taxes on the entire amount at that time, at current tax rates you still would have $677,000! You can see why the deduction of your initial contribution is not that important: $80,000 grew to $677,000 after all taxes were taken out. Does it really matter whether or not you saved a few tax dollars when you made the initial contribution?

Starting at age 59½ you can take money out of your IRA account without paying a penalty. The penalty can be severe, so think long and hard before you pull money out prior to 59½. Even if you wait and avoid the penalty, you will have to pay income taxes on the amount you withdraw, but you have two options: You can take out the total amount as a lump sum distribution as we did in the example in the previous paragraph, or you can also take out smaller amounts and simply pay taxes on the amount you withdraw.

In the first IRA example, to keep it simple, we left money in the IRA account until age 70½ and then withdrew everything. Rather than take out $975,000 in one big chunk, you should probably withdraw some money each year, not all at once. Though you do pay taxes on whatever you pull out, the balance keeps growing, tax-deferred.

At age 70½, you have to start taking money out each year.

The idea is that you completely clear out the account during a period based on an average life expectancy. For a 70-year-old, the calculation would be based on an average life expectancy of approximately 18 years. Let's see what the annual taxable income would be.

The first column in the table below shows the taxable annual income. The second shows the value of the account, which continues to grow for several years even though substantial income is taken out. And the annual income keeps going up as well.

Year	Annual Income (Taxable)	Account Value
		$ 975,000
1	$ 59,583	1,012,917
2	65,542	1,048,667
3	72,096	1,081,438
4	79,305	1,110,276
5	87,236	1,134,067
6	95,960	1,151,515
7	105,556	1,161,111
8	116,111	1,161,111
9	127,722	1,149,499
10	140,494	1,123,955
11	154,544	1,081,807
12	169,998	1,019,989
13	186,998	934,990
14	205,698	822,791
15	226,268	678,803
16	248,894	497,789
17	273,784	273,784
18	301,162	0

You can continue reaping the benefits of tax-deferred growth for many years, because the account keeps building until the eighth year, even though you are taking out a handsome annual IRA "salary." If you want to take out more than the minimum in certain years, that's entirely at your discretion. Contribute to your IRA now—you'll be very glad you did.

CORPORATE AND OTHER TYPES OF RETIREMENT PLANS: TIME TO TAKE CHARGE

Corporations, unincorporated businesses, governments, and charitable organizations can all set up retirement plans too. Once a plan is established, the contributions are deductible and the investment returns in the account grow tax-deferred. Plans differ depending on the type and size of the company or organization. A one-person vacuum cleaner repair shop will have a very different type of plan than AT&T, but the principle is the same.

The most important variable is whether your employer contributes to the plan for you, or whether you simply have the right to contribute your own money. Another important issue is the direction of investments: Does your employer handle investing, or do you have the responsibility to make those decisions?

To understand corporate retirement plans, break them down into two main categories—defined benefit and defined contribution.

Defined Benefit (Pension) Plans

Defined benefit plans are usually called pension plans. For many years, these were the most common types of retirement plans. A defined benefit plan specifies what the employee's monthly or annual benefit will be at retirement. The employer contributes an annual amount, which is invested. The combined amount, employer contributions and investment returns, is monitored to make sure enough money is accumulating to take care of employees when they retire.

Defined Contribution Plans

Defined contribution plans have several names, including profit-sharing plans, money purchase plans, Keogh plans (generally Keoghs are defined contribution, but not exclusively),

401(k) salary deferral plans, or 403(b) plans. IRAs are a form of defined contribution plan, because they are structured to allow you to put in a specific amount of money.

In a defined contribution plan, the employer sets up a separate account for each person in the plan. Money goes in and is invested as directed by the plan's trustees. Some plans leave investment control up to the trustees. Others, primarily 401(k) plans, have a menu of investment options from which participants can choose.

RETIREMENT INVESTING

Retirement plans generally take a conservative investment approach favoring safety and modest growth. Investments are generally in stocks, bonds, and cash equivalents. Some retirement plans own real estate, and others have gone into more speculative holdings such as venture capital, timber, and oil and gas deals.

In a profit-sharing plan or any other form of defined contribution plan, whatever the investment approach used, the employee simply receives the value of his or her account at retirement or upon leaving the firm. The amount the employee receives depends entirely on the dollars contributed plus accumulated investment returns.

VEST FOR SUCCESS

The term *vesting* refers to when you own the money in your retirement plan account. After a specified number of years, you have a nonforfeitable right to money in your retirement account; this is true even if you leave. Most companies require that you work for a year before you can start accumulating a share of the retirement plan. After that it takes as much as five years before you are fully vested. Of course, any cash you personally contribute is yours immediately, but the company's contribution usually is not yours until you've stayed with the firm and met the company's vesting requirements.

SELF-EMPLOYED RETIREMENT PLANS

Self-employed individuals or owners of unincorporated businesses can also set up a plan. Unincorporated plans are usually referred to as Keogh or H.R. 10 plans, but they are almost identical to corporate plans.

401(K) SALARY DEFERRAL PLANS

Many companies now have 401(k) salary deferral plans. These work much like super-IRAs—super because you can contribute up to nearly $8,000, rather than the $2,000 limit for an IRA. And you don't have to worry about the income limit for deductibility that IRAs have. In a 401(k) plan, your company puts your dollars directly into the plan where they immediately go to work. The money doesn't even appear— or get taxed—on your paycheck. This means you don't have income taxes withheld from your savings in the plan. And, in many cases, your employer will contribute an additional amount as a match for all or a portion of your contribution. When you put in your contribution, you get a bonus that will make your account grow even faster.

For example, if your employer's matching contribution is 10 percent, when you put in $3,000 your employer puts in $300; you get an automatic 10 percent return. (Contributing to the 401(k) plan won't reduce your social security benefits when you retire because the same amount of social security (FICA) taxes will be deducted from your salary whether you contribute or not.)

MEET MARY ANN; SHE'S PLANNING AHEAD WITH A 401(K)

Let's take a look at a typical person, Mary Ann, who earns $30,000 a year. She's married, and she and her husband Ed file a joint tax return. Mary Ann decides to contribute 10 percent of her pay, or $3,000. Now you're probably saying, "On $30,000 a year she can't afford to contribute $3,000, right?" Wrong. Keep reading.

At current rates, Mary Ann and Ed's federal income tax (to simplify things, we are ignoring state and local income taxes) would, at current rates, be about $3,246. Thus, spendable income would be $26,754.

By making a $3,000 tax-deferred contribution to the 401(k) plan, Mary Ann reduces taxable income by $3,000, from $30,000 to $27,000. This cuts the Federal income tax bite by $450 to $2,796 leaving spendable income of $24,204. Let's see what happens to the $3,000 tax-deferred contribution she makes each year. Instead of airmailing some of that money to the tax collector in Washington, D.C., she's got it working for her future, not Uncle Sam's deficit reduction program.

When Mary Ann contributed her $3,000, her employer added a matching contribution of $300 to raise the account balance $3,300. Lets look at the running totals:

	With 401(k)	Without 401(k)
Gross income	$30,000	$30,000
401(k) contribution	3,000	0
Taxable income	27,000	30,000
Taxes (federal)	2,796	3,246
Spendable income	24,204	26,754
401(k)	3,300	0
Total	27,504	26,754

To keep it simple, I have ignored all of the normal deductions one might take. Adding back the 401(k) balance to the bottom line is also a bit simplistic, because it ignores the fact that she will have to pay taxes on that amount. But remember, the 401(k) account is her money and it's growing, tax-deferred, for her future.

Let's see how the account grows over time as she continues contributing, getting occasional pay raises, receiving the

	Account Balance
Year 1	$ 3,630
Year 5 (End-of-year promotion and salary increase to $35,000.)	22,162
Year 10 (Promotion and salary increase to $40,000.)	61,546
Year 15 (Promotion and salary increase to $45,000.)	128,670
Year 20 (Promotion and salary increase to $50,000.)	240,466
Year 25 (Promotion and salary increase to $55,000.)	424,209
Year 30 (Retirement.)	723,823

matching contribution from her employer, and earning 10 percent in the account. As she receives pay increases, she also increases the dollar amount of the contribution to keep it at 10 percent.

By tightening her belt a little bit, Mary Ann built up a big nest egg. It's true, she had to give up spending a few thousand dollars each year, but for that she earned tax-deferred savings worth $723,823.

No matter what your situation is, if you work for a living—part or full-time—you can do the same thing. Now let's see what happens when Mary Ann retires.

TAX DECISION: IRA ROLLOVER VERSUS LUMP SUM

Lump sum: Chinese food served all at once. Just kidding—I wanted to see if there was life behind those rapidly glazing eyes.

When she retires, Mary Ann may be able to keep her money in the 401(k) for a year or so, but she will eventually have to take it out. Upon retiring, many people choose to roll the money into what's known as an IRA rollover account. This allows the retiring employee avoid paying taxes on the entire amount because it is in another tax-deferred plan, the IRA rollover.

Under current law, another option is a lump sum distribution. This option offers favorable tax treatment at reduced rates. The question of using an IRA rollover account versus taking a lump sum distribution is complex. Because tax laws change every year, you should get advice from a certified public accountant or a tax attorney. Spend a little money for professional tax advice; it's worth it.

If you choose the lump sum option, you simply pay the taxes and that's that. Though the IRA rollover option is a little more complicated, for many people it's the better choice.

IT'S YOUR MONEY, SO ASK THE HARD QUESTIONS

No matter where you work, look into your retirement plan. Find out what type of plan you have. To find out more about your retirement benefits, first see who handles this area in your company. In small organizations, you should talk to your boss. If you work for a larger company, there probably is a personnel or human resources department in charge of the plan. Sometimes the treasurer or controller or vice president of finance is the main company officer handling the retirement plan. Whoever it is, that person can explain to you exactly how your plan works and what options you have.

With your investments, time is your ally. Physically, passing years usually bring us a wrinkle or two and a few more gray hairs—perhaps even fewer hairs. Also, there's probably more of you to love than there was 10 or 20 years ago. But if you contribute to a retirement plan, along with a spreading waistline you can get a beautiful, bulging bottom line.

10

Huddling with the Pros: Take Their Smartest Strategies and Navigate the Road to Investment Success

The first investment pro, Robert Fleming, set high standards, which are still alive today in the pros you're about to meet. These hard workers seek out and analyze investments day after day, year upon year. They read voraciously, crunch numbers, and dig and dig until they have unearthed something of lasting value.

Most spent a long apprenticeship learning their trade. Frank Cappiello began working as a research analyst in 1962, several years before Mario Gabelli signed on at Loeb Rhodes. Claude Rosenberg and Jack Leylegian began honing their skills in the late 1950s. Steve Lieber started on Wall Street in the late 1940s. Mike Price, the youngest of the group, came to Wall Street in 1972, and Roy Neuberger, the oldest, started in 1929, seven months before the stock market crashed. (Roy's interview is the longest of the seven mutual fund pros. I thought you would enjoy a more complete picture of his life.)

Each, through hard, personal effort, intuition, and trial and error, has developed an investment style—a signature method of handcrafting an investment portfolio. Over the years of bull markets and bad ones, they have refined their craft through rigorous testing and difficult trials in the battle for investment success.

Though similarities exist, each is convinced that his method, his style is the best—and it is, for him. Though their techniques may differ, many of the underlying themes are the same. Let's go meet them.

INTERVIEW: FRANK CAPPIELLO

If you've watched *Wall $treet Week*, you've seen Frank Cappiello. He's the chatty panel member with the long, mournful face. He's not really sad, though, just thoughtful.

Cappiello is the president of a swiftly growing investment management firm, McCullough, Andrews, and Cappiello, headquartered in San Francisco. The firm, which also has an office in Baltimore, manages over $1 billion for retirement plans, trusts, and individuals. Cappiello also manages two mutual funds, Carnegie-Cappiello Growth Fund and Carnegie-Capiello Total Return Fund, from his base in Baltimore.

After graduating from Notre Dame in South Bend, Indiana, Cappiello went directly into the Marines, serving with an automatic weapons battalion as a first lieutenant. When he came out of the service, at first he intended to go to law school, but his battalion commander convinced him to go to Harvard Business School. He figured Cappiello's personality needed the excitement and financial rewards of business.

Graduating from Harvard, a freshly minted M.B.A. in hand, he went to work for an electric utility, Virginia Electric Power. At that time, utilities were a real growth industry, and Cappiello's career was promising. But the bubbling stock market of 1961 drew him like a magnet to Wall Street.

Cappiello went to work for Alex Brown & Company in Baltimore, Maryland, and then he spent several years managing investments for a large life insurance company.

Now, between his management duties at McCullough, Andrews, and Cappiello and his public appearances on *Wall $treet Week* and elsewhere, Frank stays very busy, but he did find time to co-author *From Main St. to Wall St.: Making Money in Real Estate*, with Karl McClennan.

Brouwer: Frank, let's talk about your mutual fund. It has two portfolios—growth and total return. Do you have a preference or feel more comfortable with one of those styles?

Cappiello: The styles are not that different. You know, there are only a handful of styles on Wall Street.

Brouwer: What are some of them?

Cappiello: One of them is growth. It could be buying the classic growth companies like IBM, or an alternative method is investing in smaller, emerging companies like Compaq Computer. Another important investment style is income, and you get income through high-yielding stocks or bonds, CDs, and so on. In the total return portfolio we are combining growth and income in one portfolio. In the other portfolio, it's aiming at pure growth. In growth, we look for companies that are increasing their earnings per share. Earnings show that a company has done a number of things right—a good return on investment, market share, position of the company in its marketplace, and a lot of other things. One of the things I look for in a total return approach is growth, too, but the growth objective there is much more modest. What you're looking for there is growth in earnings that will provide for an increase in the dividend. So, the techniques are basic bread and butter, it's just the seasonings, the salt and pepper, that are a little different.

Brouwer: Aren't you more comfortable with one or the other?

Cappiello: Over the years, I think people tend to make the most money with mutual funds that invest primarily in growth stocks. However, you've got to be comfortable taking a fair amount of risk.

Brouwer: Right. You have to learn to ride the ups and downs.

Cappiello: Exactly. Market cycles can kill you. The way to make money in mutual funds is to use compounding, and the compounding takes effect when you have a good return and you keep on plowing that back into more and more shares.

Brouwer: Most people think you need to take a lot of risk to get a good return, but modest returns can grow rapidly with compounding.

Cappiello: To make money, first make sure you don't lose it. Because if you go down fifty percent, you have to double to make the money back, and that's pretty hard to do.

Brouwer: How should an investor focus on his or her optimum investment objectives and asset mix?

Cappiello: If you want growth, I think it makes sense to buy into a good growth mutual fund that invests in technology, drug companies, consumer goods, and a few more. Stocks like Merck, Syntex, Sears, and so on.

Brouwer: Beyond growth funds, what's next?

Cappiello: Salt and pepper. Some seasoning. That extra pizzazz. Seriously, I would say that 20 percent should be in a mutual fund that specializes in small company stocks. This is where you're trying for the home run.

Brouwer: A home run? With all the salt and seasoning, I thought we were cooking. After the small company fund, what's next?

Cappiello: Remember the old 80/20 rule? Eighty percent of your winners are going to come from 20 percent of the mutual funds. Unfortunately, you don't know which of your mutual funds are going to be the winners.

Brouwer: Do you think an individual with, say, $50,000, or even $500,000, can do better buying individual stocks and bonds than buying several mutual funds?

Cappiello: Only if they're willing to pay the price.

Brouwer: If they're willing to put in a lot of time.

Cappiello: Right. It has to be a way of life. People say you can just spend an hour a day or two on stocks, but that's false. You've got to live it. In order for it to work, it really has to be an avocation, like playing tennis or stamp collecting. It's something that is going to consume a lot of your free time. You've got to like it. You've got to have greed, you have to have patience, you've got to have emotional stability. But if you have all of those factors pulling together, hell, that's the way I started.

Brouwer: What's most important?

Cappiello: The emotional mix; you can't have any emotional baggage. One of the rules is to diversify. But the second rule is, Never look back. Yesterday's stock market is yesterday's stock market. You just move on. Otherwise, you get all frustrated.

Brouwer: You talk about that in your next book, don't you?

Cappiello: That's right. We have a chapter on personal motivation. It's like a computer. It's got all of the data, but you still have to turn it on. Controlling your emotions becomes a lot easier after you've had a couple of successes and develop some financial security.

Brouwer: Each buy or sell decision isn't a life or death matter. What do you think about people who claim they can predict the market week in and week out?

Cappiello: Short-term market timing and telephone switch newsletters (advisory services that recommend the use of mutual fund families that allow investors to switch out of one fund into another with a phone call) are ridiculous. I've seen their track records and most of them are sheer, unadulterated crap.

Brouwer: Don't sugarcoat it, Frank, get it off your chest.

Cappiello: I've seen dozens and dozens try, and I've only seen a handful who had any success at all calling market turns. Calling the market, picking the specific industry group that leads the way—that is the most difficult of them all.

Brouwer: A few telephone switch newsletters have had fine records, but most have not. If we agree that telephone switch formats are not the only way to go, what is?

Cappiello: If you believe the market is going up, buy the quality funds.

Brouwer: Buying a good growth fund that's investing in stocks with good earnings and so on.

Cappiello: Yes. In a poor market you can average down, but I personally would rather average up in a rising market. When things are working well, buy more. Ninety percent of the people don't buy on the way up, but the 10 percent that do are the people who really make the money. But if you want to bottom-fish, eventually all or most battered funds will have their day.

Brouwer: Can you give us a recent example?

Cappiello: A year ago, you could have bought the oils—the energy funds. They owned Texaco, Atlantic Richfield, Chevron, and so on. At that time, most people were saying oil could go to $8 a barrel. Sure. And a comet can hit the earth. Worst-case situations always get the press. Buying what's out of favor is a steady way of making money.

Brouwer: What's the best way for investors to learn?

Cappiello: Get some basic investing knowledge. Take a course in security analysis. Most cities, no matter how big or small, have a summer course or even a course during the regular sessions. You need that course. If you take a good, solid course with a good textbook, you'll know about 80 percent of what Wall Streeters keep in the back of their mind. You won't know the other 20 percent, which is experience and precious, hard-earned detail.

Brouwer: Do you believe in technical analysis (the analysis of market and individual stock past performance charts in order to divine future movements)?

Cappiello: No. It doesn't work. However, 5,000 people on Wall Street practice it. They can make it reality for a while. So you should get to know what they see in a certain chart pattern.

Brouwer: At times, major chart patterns can be a self-fulfilling prophecy—at least for a little while.

Cappiello: That's right. Out of self-protection, I study charts. Cycles don't repeat exactly. And that's what kills pure chartists.

Brouwer: How many funds should an investor have?

Cappiello: Six would be enough.

Brouwer: How would you go about looking at mutual funds for people of different ages?

Cappiello: Young people should focus on growth, almost exclusively. Twenty percent in mutual funds that buy smaller rapidly growing companies. An example of that would be the OTC Fund or T. Rowe Price's New Horizons Fund. Then another 20 percent in aggressive growth. Possibly international, but I'm very skeptical about that run continuing. International funds' current popularity is simply because they had a nice streak for the past three years. But streaks tend to flatten out.

Brouwer: How about middle-aged people?

Cappiello: That would be a combination of growth mutual funds plus balanced growth and income. And you begin to scale down your growth, to move some of that to growth plus income, more the total return package.

Brouwer: How do you feel about gold?

Cappiello: I'd certainly have 10 percent in gold.

Brouwer: Why do you say that?

Cappiello: Simply because at some point you need a hedge. And this is a hedge against the worst thing happening for the average individual or anyone, and that is losing your money and having to start all over again. I don't think we're going to have a 1929 again, at least not in my lifetime. It won't develop that way. But we could have a financial cataclysm that could hurt all of us. If you have 10 percent in gold, the other 90 percent can go down the

tubes and you'll still be okay. That assumes everyone is
in bad shape, and your 10 percent will allow you to start
over again because everyone else has been savaged. And
that's the whole game of gold. You really want to hope that
it doesn't work. People misunderstand gold. They think
they have to be 30 and 40 percent in gold, or they have
to switch around, and you don't. The time to have gold is
when you don't want it. Because when the time comes to
have gold, everyone will have run the price of gold up.

Brouwer: I'm still not convinced. Just because gold went up
in the last depression, that doesn't mean it will this time
around. But assuming someone wants gold, what's the
best way? Bullion, coins, gold mining shares, gold teeth,
gold mutual funds?

Cappiello: Gold mutual funds.

Brouwer: When they retire, many people put all their money
in CDs or Treasury bills. Does this make sense?

Cappiello: No, you need some growth and income stocks or
mutual funds.

Brouwer: I think a lot of people make the mistake of becoming overly conservative at retirement.

Cappiello: They stop the investment battle. But the battle
never ends because your enemy is the government and
inflation. It's either inflation trying to take the money
away from you in a subtle way or the government trying
to take money away in taxes. In either case, it's a battle
to maintain your lifestyle. Your purchasing power. If you
retire at age 70, you might live to be 90.

Brouwer: What would be a good mix for someone who's 60,
65—already retired or thinking about it?

Cappiello: Now you move from growth funds to more balanced mutual funds, investing in both stocks and bonds.

Brouwer: In other words, the older investor should be more
conservative, but not completely income-oriented.

Cappiello: Yes. We would shift exclusively to total return
type mutual funds. In particular, funds that focus on
utilities or convertible bonds.

Brouwer: They'd still have a fairly high percentage in stocks, but they would be more conservative ones.

Cappiello: That's right. In addition, they should have some bonds or bond funds, some gold funds, and money in a money market fund or a bank.

Brouwer: Sounds good. Earlier, we talked a little bit about real estate stocks. Do you think people should put money into real estate investment trusts (REITs)?

Cappiello: Absolutely. In fact, I think that would make a great mutual fund—I think there's a hell of a fund idea in that.

Brouwer: There are a couple of them now.

Cappiello: True. But there's always room for a very good one.

And there's always room for good investment ideas. Cappiello knows the stock market moves in cycles. But no matter how high it soars or how low it falls, the same standards of value and common sense have to be used. Values don't change.

Cappiello says the way to make money in the market is to take advantage of compounding—steady growth. And you must always look forward, never back; saying "I should have or could have" is self-destructive. He also bluntly points out that most short-term market timing and telephone switch newsletters are "sheer, unadulterated crap." And if you are retired, remember you still need growth to keep up with inflation.

Frank uses solid, proven investment strategies and techniques to build wealth for his clients. You can do the same for your clients—you and your family.

INTERVIEW: MICHAEL PRICE

Mike Price is the president of the Mutual Series Fund and the successor to Max Heine, one of Wall Street's legendary investors. Mutual Series has three portfolios—Shares, Qualified, and Beacon. The investment style—searching for undervalued investments—is the same for all three. But Shares and Qualified are closed. Beacon is open ($50,000 minimum, but only $2,000 for IRAs). This habit of closing and reopening the fund periodically can be both confusing and annoying if you've been shut out. Hopefully, they will soon reopen to new investors.

The Mutual Series Fund, founded in 1949, has compiled a superb record—achieving above-average returns in up markets and preserving investor capital in down markets. For example, in 1973 and 1974, the S & P 500 plunged 37 percent. Many mutual funds dropped as much as 50 percent in that agonizing 18-month period. But Mutual Series was only down 8 percent in 1973 and it was actually up 8 percent in 1974. For the two-year period, Mutual Series investors broke even. Similarly, the funds performed well on Black Monday, October 19, 1987, holding up well on the worst day in stock market history. This ability to preserve capital in weak markets, along with the funds' solid performance in strong markets, has given them a superb record over many years. It hasn't hurt business either; the family of three funds now has billions in assets.

Several years ago, I asked Heine how he was able to beat the Street, going up in 1974 when most funds dropped like wounded birds. In his crisp German accent he said, "Our stocks were so bad, they couldn't go down no more." He was referring to the fact that many of their investments were in companies Wall Street had given up on.

Mike Price and I met for this interview during trading hours, and Price was all business. He got off the first question: "How long will this take?" Once started, though, he talked freely and openly about his philosophy.

Brouwer: When did you start with Mutual Series?

Price: The end of 1974.

Brouwer: How did you happen to start working here?

Price: During college I had a summer job with a former partner of Max Heine's. But when I graduated in 1973, no one on Wall Street was hiring. Finally I got on with a firm I had worked for in college, during the summer. I stayed there a year. And one of the people who left that firm joined Max and mentioned that Max was looking for someone to follow special situation stocks. Mutual Shares then had about $5 million in it. At the very end of 1974, I joined with him. In August of 1975, Max took over full management of the fund and we worked together from then on.

Brouwer: It's amazing; Mutual Shares only had $5 million?

Price: By the time I started, maybe it was $6 million. We had a good year in 1975 and a great one in 1976. That was during the Penn Central bankruptcy [a spectacular railroad bankruptcy from the early seventies] and the market was very cheap. It seemed like everything we bought went up. In 1976, the fund was up something like 55 percent. After that three-year period our performance numbers started showing up in magazines and other places where people check mutual fund performance. Then money started coming in.

Brouwer: Now you have a large trading room and a big staff. How many of you were there then?

Price: Just the two of us. It's only been in the last couple of years that we hired other analysts. Now we have 12 analysts, and 55 people all together.

Brouwer: How much do you have in the three funds?

Price: We have $5 billion in the three mutual funds. And we're still doing the exact same things we did with $6 million.

Brouwer: How did you guys find one investment strategy you could stick to through all types of markets?

Price: Well, it's not one, we really do three things.

Brouwer: What are the three strategies?

Price: Max has been investing in bankrupt companies since the 1930s. He also has a great nose for cheap stocks. Stocks that represent far more intrinsic value than they're selling for.

Brouwer: That's two.

Price: And I came in with the arbitrage deals, takeovers. [Traditionally, *arbitrage* means the simultaneous buying and selling of an investment on different exchanges to take advantage of small differences in price. Risk arbitrage is essentially investing in companies that are the object of takeover offers.] I also have a good feel for what we call liquidations [the dissolution and sale of all of a company's assets]—companies worth more dead than alive.

Brouwer: So the investments in the funds actually represent three approaches. What's an example of each?

Price: An example of a bankruptcy or reorganization is Storage Technology, which is currently coming out of Chapter 11 [bankruptcy]. We own quite a bit of it, a position we bought some time ago. We bought it when no one wanted to take the risk.

Brouwer: What about an example of a cheap stock?

Price: In the recent market collapse we saw so many cheap stocks, you can't single one out.

Brouwer: I suppose United would be an example of the arbitrage method.

Price: Yes. We invested in it because we thought the sum of the parts was worth much more than the stock was selling for.

Brouwer: Well, that idea certainly worked.

Price: These disciplines fit well together. After several years, we realized that the portfolio had a third of its money in cheap stocks, a third in arbitrage or takeover deals, and a third in bankruptcies, liquidations, and cash equivalents.

Brouwer: And you've stuck to that formula?

Price: Yes. Because when the market got hurt, our funds still did well. And when the market did fine, the fund kept going along nicely.

Brouwer: It's very unusual that you have a lot of your funds' assets in things that are not particularly liquid. For example, the large position in R.H. Macy & Company. Because it is a privately held company, the stock doesn't trade in the public market. This means it is less liquid because it would take a lot of time to convert that holding into cash equivalents. Most mutual funds don't do that.

Price: Ninety percent of the portfolio is very liquid. The other 10 percent is really different and terrific. We noticed that in corporate bankruptcy proceedings, banks often wanted to sell out at any cost. So we bought bank loans and corporate debts at a huge discount to their real value. We bought them cheaper than comparable publicly held bonds. The investments made terrific sense, so we asked our shareholders to approve these kinds of things.

With Storage Technology, we bought mortgages and loans from 11 banks. We were paying an average of $500 for a loan with a principal amount of $1,000. At the same time, the same company's bonds traded at $600, $700. And our bank loans were safer than the publicly held bonds. It turns out we'll make almost three times our investment on some of these investments, and we had very little risk when we did it.

Brouwer: Is anybody else doing this?

Price: Not in mutual funds, because it's not easy to do. It's a lot of work. A few other people do it on Wall Street, but they do it in a much smaller way. Because of our size, we can put more money into a situation than anyone else. So the banks come to us, which gives us a negotiating edge.

Brouwer: To change the subject, since your investment policy is to be more conservative as the stock market moves higher, how do you accomplish that?

Price: We're keeping a lot of our assets in Treasury bills and other very short-term investments. During periods when the market moves higher and higher, we move progressively more into cash equivalents. Today we're at 20 percent.

Brouwer: That's a high level of cash for you, isn't it?

Price: Yes, it is. But you've got to stay liquid the next couple of years. We've had one panic and there will probably be more. We want to be prepared for opportunities and the only way to be prepared is to have cash on the sidelines.

Brouwer: Do you invest in your own funds?

Price: Sure. I own all of my funds. So does Max.

Brouwer: If you weren't buying your own mutual funds, whose would you buy?

Price: I'd buy Steve Lieber's funds [the Evergreen Fund and the Evergreen Total Return Fund]. I'd buy Mario Gabelli's mutual fund, the Gabelli Fund.

Brouwer: Are there any other funds you like?

Price: Well, I think what Peter Lynch did with the Magellan Fund was brilliant. I also like the Sequoia Fund, but that's closed to new investors. So there aren't that many out there that I like.

Brouwer: Are there too many funds now?

Price: Absolutely. Look at the number of funds that only have a one- two- or three-year record. The effect of unseasoned management can be brutal in bear markets.

Brouwer: What should investors do to preserve capital when the market is up towards the higher end of its historical value?

Price: Stay relatively defensive. Keep a fair amount in U.S. Treasury bills or CDs at solid banks and savings and loans.

Brouwer: What should investors stay away from?

Price: Becoming overly aggressive. Doing things like buying Australian bonds with high interest rates. The Japanese, Korean, and Taiwan markets, those sorts of things.

Brouwer: Are you against investing in foreign stocks?

Price: Not at all. We have done very well in Lonhro and Rio Tinto Zinc, two stocks on the London Exchange. For three years we've had a guy working for us who is a specialist in foreign stocks. Recently, we had 12 percent of our portfolio in foreign stocks.

Brouwer: Is size becoming a problem? The amount of money in the funds?

Price: Is it a problem? Yes and no. Size makes you bigger and makes you able to do bigger things. You see more deals because of that. Size also dilutes your good ideas. Dilutes your bad ideas. I think right now we're okay. If we went to $5 billion, it would be a problem. Our performance so far is fine. The bottom line is, you have to make a number of very large bets each year to keep your returns up. We make $50 million or $100 million bets. When you do that, you've got to be right.

Brouwer: Did you have a problem with massive redemptions when the market dropped?

Price: No. We had very few redemptions—two to three percent. But many funds had a big problem, particularly those favored by market timers and telephone switch newsletters.

Brouwer: What about all the new funds who have inexperienced people running them?

Price: You need someone in business for five years or more to see if they know what they're doing over a market cycle. Until October 1987, we had five years of up markets, so you can't distinguish real quality. There's a lot of money in mutual funds being run by people who don't know what they're doing. Market corrections help weed the inexperienced out.

Brouwer: How can somebody do a better job of finding out who's good?

Price: You read the publications. You work at it. *Consumer Reports* just did this story on a risk-adjusted mutual fund method. Then look at the *Forbes* Honor Roll. There are many services you can subscribe to. But you have to go with the ones you understand and believe in.

Brouwer: We talked a little bit about emotions in investing. Most people's emotions hurt their investment performance. How do you avoid becoming overly emotional?

Price: It's very hard. There are a couple of emotions, you know. There's the gut feeling, which is the good kind of emotion, that it smells right to you. And that's a real important part of what we do here; it's got to feel right. You have a conviction, but your gut has to tell you it's right. But there's the bad side, when you fall in love with the stock, and you don't sell it when it's overvalued, or you buy it and buy it and buy it as it goes lower and lower.

Brouwer: So emotions can get in your way?

Price: That's right. You have to stick to real values, and you have to wait until you have solid facts to go with your good instincts—gut feelings.

Brouwer: I've found that whenever I go against my instincts, it's usually a mistake. Are most investors doomed to buy high and sell low? Can people change their emotional response?

Price: There was a quote in the paper about the Japanese market. Their attitude is that if everyone crosses the street when the light's red, no one's going to get hit. That's stupid. Reality will set in. Investors simply have to discipline themselves to sell when other people are buying. At Mutual Shares, our natural instinct is to do the opposite of the Street. Great news comes out, we sell into it. We buy stocks after they file for bankruptcy. We love to buy on bad news.

Brouwer: Can the ordinary investor trade stocks competitively?

Price: It's impossible for the small investor to trade stocks— impossible. You've got to be there every day. It requires a lot of time and reading. Most investors don't even read the *Wall Street Journal.* Investing is a full-time job, there's no question about it. I work, not only full-time in the office, but full-time at home.

Brouwer: How much time do you work each week? How many hours?

Price: Maybe 14 or 15 a day. On weekends a few. And when we're real busy, I'll spend more on the weekend.

Brouwer: So what time do you get up in the morning?

Price: Five twenty. Drive in at six, six fifteen. I get here at seven thirty, eight o'clock. In the car I have a phone, so I call London to see what's doing. Driving along I can talk to the office. I leave at four fifteen, get home at five thirty, play with the kids, eat some dinner, and then I put in a few hours at home. I have a computer with the Dow Jones market manager program, so I have access to all the news items. I can do searches on several databases. I do earnings forecasting. Look at brokerage research reports.

Brouwer: Do you ever foresee a time when you don't want to do that any more?

Price: No, I enjoy doing that. The only question is do you want to do it with 23 people, to have to manage the people and the office. I have to worry about $3 billion for 150,000 people. At some point, I may just decide to work simply for my own account. But I like doing what we do, and I like the size of it, because we can do some significant investments.

Brouwer: What's the most important quality for a good portfolio manager?

Price: People have to be able to talk to you. And you have to make decisions on your feet, right on the spot. You can't just take it all in and regurgitate it.

Brouwer: You don't have five weeks to think it over.

Price: No, I mean, you've got to make decisions—pull the trigger. I started making decisions the second week. Max didn't pay any attention to me. So, I figured I'll come up with some ideas. I worked on 10 deals. Told him the best three and he bought one of them. I quickly understood what he was looking for. So I only gave him the good ones, and he developed confidence in me pretty quickly. In the first or second year, I started trading for the fund, and from 1976 to 1977, Max and I were running it together.

Brouwer: With Max slowing down, how do you handle the work?

Price: Now, I have seven analysts who come to me with ideas. As each one develops the ability to make investment decisions that are clearly our style, I let him take more responsibility. That way, they really look forward to coming to work because they can put their ideas to the test.

Brouwer: In other words, to have portfolio management responsibilities, a research analyst has to be able to find superb investments, but he also needs street smarts.

Price: That's right. We have some good traders who have weak analytical abilities and good analytical people who have very poor trading judgment. Then we have one or two who do have nice combinations. It's difficult to get it all in one person, someone I can get along with, someone I trust, who can make decisions for trading and also decisions on other things. You know, that's a lot to expect in one person—brains and great instincts.

It's so true that brilliant analysts often lack decisiveness—they can't pull the trigger. And street-smart traders often shoot from the hip. Perhaps having those skills in one person made the difference for Mutual Series. For years, the person at the helm—first Max Heine and now Mike Price—has been both smart and decisive.

Mike Price single-mindedly concentrates on specialized investments. He works—and has worked since 1974—14 or 15 hours a day. In addition to having great personal drive and ability, he had the opportunity to learn his trade under Max Heine, one of the top investment pros of the past 50 years.

Price believes the key to Mutual Series' success is a three-pronged investment strategy—they buy bankruptcies, undervalued stocks, and certain takeover candidates. They venture into backwaters of the investment business that scare off other investors, turning trash into treasure. Another valuable trait is the ability to recognize and deal with mistakes. Everyone makes them, but winners turn them around quickly. This combination of three separate investment strategies and old-fashioned hard work has made them successful. It couldn't hurt you either.

INTERVIEW: STEPHEN LIEBER

Stephen Lieber is the founder and chairman of the top-rated Evergreen Fund and the Evergreen Total Return Fund. His firm also has started a new fund, the Evergreen Value Timing Fund. Lieber's firm manages a total of $3.8 billion for over 200,000 investors.

Lieber looks and talks more like a philosophy professor than a numbers-driven mutual fund portfolio manager. He graduated from tiny Williams College, in Williamstown, Massachusetts, with a degree in English, not business or economics. And he *is* an academic; his successful career has been built on a rigorous program of disciplined research and meticulous investment analysis.

The genesis of his research methods dates back to 1950, when he took some time off from Harvard Graduate School of Arts and Sciences to toil away as a research assistant and part-time broker for a municipal bond firm. He was dissatisfied with the narrow focus of this work, even though he loved Wall Street itself. He then went to work for another, more broadly based brokerage firm, called Oppenheimer Vandenbroek & Company, analyzing stocks to find those that were undervalued. Before long, graduate school was forgotten.

Lieber moved onward and upward to become a partner in 1954. In 1956, along with three other partners, he set up shop for himself. But by 1969, the firm's success had become a two-edged sword; Lieber was slogging away, becoming increasingly embroiled in administration and office politics, not research and portfolio management—his first love.

He felt the answer was to get away from Wall Street, with its frantic enthusiasms and pushy sales campaigns designed to tout high-flying stocks. Lieber particularly wanted out of the clubby, old-boy network of lunches and meetings with other Wall Streeters, because he believed they promoted the herd mentality, not original thinking. His partners disagreed. In 1969, at age 43, he set up his own firm, Lieber & Company.

Two years later, he started his first mutual fund, the Evergreen Fund. His second fund, the Evergreen Total Return Fund, began in 1978. Now, he is nurturing his latest mutual fund, the Evergreen Value Timing Fund. Both the Evergreen Fund and the Evergreen Total Return Fund have been perennial top performers.

Both Mike Price (Mutual Series Fund) and Jack Leylegian (Leylegian Investment Management) told me they think Evergreen Fund has a superb record.

Brouwer: Your two most well-known funds are the Evergreen Fund and the Evergreen Total Return Fund. What's the difference between them?

Lieber: They each focus on a different spectrum of investment opportunity. Both have very simple objectives. In the Total Return Fund we have two objectives—a 20 percent annual return coupled with lower downside risk than the stock and bond market averages.

Brouwer: That doesn't sound that simple to me. What are the objectives for the Evergreen Fund?

Lieber: In the Evergreen Fund we have a target rate of return of 30 percent, but with higher risk or volatility than the market as a whole. In the Evergreen Fund, we also want to be in companies with entrepreneurial management, because we believe that is the fastest-growing business sector.

Brouwer: The Total Return concept is more conservative?

Lieber: With the Total Return concept of investing in high-yielding stocks, there is a limited downside risk. They just don't have that much market risk. In addition, we have a strong sell discipline when the market moves up.

Brouwer: What about sell discipline for the Evergreen Fund?

Lieber: With the Evergreen Fund, it's different. We have an automatic program to review any stock that is down

10 percent. If a stock goes down further, we know our original analysis was wrong, and we have to take a hard look at it.

Brouwer: How do you eliminate ego from the sell decision?

Lieber: When a stock goes down, it's critical to realize an error has been made. The original analysis was wrong, period.

Brouwer: How do you decide to sell a stock?

Lieber: It varies with the type of stock and the objectives of the particular mutual fund. I was talking to one of our analysts this morning. A stock she liked had gone down, even though she still liked the company's products, business prospects, and management.

Brouwer: If everything's so good, why is the stock going down?

Lieber: That's exactly what I said. If the products are good, business is good, and management is good, why have their earnings been bad? Something is wrong with our analysis, so we'd better review it and see if we should sell out and take our loss.

Brouwer: What about asset mix? How do you decide what's an appropriate balance between stocks, bonds, and cash equivalents?

Lieber: We're basically stock market investors, so we concentrate on finding stocks that meet our standards for value and yield. We use convertible stocks and bonds quite a bit. They are a way to go if you want both yield and the potential for capital appreciation. In the Total Return Fund, we view yield as our downside protection. Periodically, when the market is high, we cut back in areas that have become fully valued, and we try to focus on the most undervalued sectors.

Brouwer: That theory was borne out on Black Monday, as Total Return went down far less than the market overall.

Lieber: That's true. But it's hard to be pleased about such a difficult period, in spite of the fact that we beat the market that day.

Brouwer: Investment styles go in and out. For much of 1987, the Total Return Fund's emphasis on high-yielding stocks was out of the market mainstream. As most people pay attention to short-term performance, they see other funds outperforming for a quarter or two, and they then dump your fund. Do you ever feel short-term performance pressure?

Lieber: Sure I do.

Brouwer: How do you deal with it?

Lieber: I try to be responsive and not get caught up in short-term trends. We could shift gears and try to tag along, but we don't because we recognize that it would be an abrupt change in our investment philosophy.

Brouwer: So you're saying, I'm willing to lag behind a wild bull market for a while, because I think it will come to an end.

Lieber: That's right.

Brouwer: One thing I admire about your philosophy is that you use investment concepts that almost anyone could grasp.

Lieber: We look for simple opportunities, but we then take great pains to make sure our analysis is sound.

Brouwer: Earlier, we talked about short-term competitive pressure. If your mutual fund is underperforming the market, then people criticize you or even leave your mutual fund. If you—an experienced, successful portfolio manager—if you feel this pressure, then less secure managers are probably in trouble.

Lieber: That's especially true of people who are under pressure from a boss at a large family of funds. The investor has to wonder if a fund is being run by investment people who are free to act on their best judgment, or are they under economic pressures from management.

Brouwer: How would someone find that out?

Lieber: You can see whether it's an independent firm or a large corporate giant; that's important. If it is a large fund family, then you need to make sure they have experienced people who have enough freedom to do their job.

Brouwer: Unfortunately, the large families of funds move portfolio managers around so much it's hard to know who is managing a particular fund.

Lieber: Yes, that's true. I could use that thought as a plug for our firm but I won't.

Brouwer: Right. Why do you think there is an increased trend to load funds now?

Lieber: It's an easy buck. We could have done it.

Brouwer: You probably had people begging you to do it.

Lieber: We have a lot of people soliciting us to do 12b-1 payments. They [brokers and financial planners can receive payments under the 12b-1 plans mentioned in Chapter 3] want a kickback from us.

Brouwer: And I'm sure investment banking firms would love to do a new offering of a mutual fund where you manage the money. That way they could earn an $8\frac{1}{2}$ percent load by touting your track record.

Lieber: Sure.

Brouwer: Why didn't you go for the money, by adding a load to your funds like Fidelity has on many of their funds?

Lieber: I just didn't feel right about it. We're well paid, but we're not greedy. In 1986, a billion dollars poured into the Total Return Fund in a short time. It would have been very easy to tack on a sales charge. Maybe the cash inflow would have dropped a little, but probably not much.

Brouwer: Not many people would give up that type of money. Why did you?

Lieber: From a pure business point of view, it may seem silly to give it up. But all I can say is that, at least we have clients and others who appreciate what we've been doing. And as time goes on, we will have other investment vehicles available. Hopefully, investors will remember they got a fair shake here. And we, on the other hand, won't feel we've taken advantage of our investors the way some firms have.

Brouwer: Getting back to the art of investing, emotions are such an important part of the process. Did your emotions ever lead you into a trap?

Lieber: The biggest blunder I ever made was letting a stock get to be too big as a percentage of our portfolios. And, of course, then it collapsed.

Brouwer: What did you learn from that?

Lieber: First, don't let too large a percentage develop in any stock. It can be dangerous. Second, neither individual stocks nor the market as a whole goes up forever.

Brouwer: When magazines print performance numbers, your funds usually look very good. Many investors pick the top-performing funds because they think they will naturally do well in the future. Do you think performance numbers have predictive value for the future?

Lieber: Performance numbers have predictive value when they are looked at in context. There are people whose market savvy only works in certain types of markets. They can look very good for a while, but it doesn't last.

Brouwer: In other words, only put faith in track records that have gone through both up and down markets.

Lieber: Yes. For example, some mutual fund groups used to start a new fund, but they would only promote them if they did well, and they would quietly fold them up if they didn't. So the track record didn't mean much. And there are a lot of very good managers who are hot for a while, and then they drop out of sight.

Brouwer: To be good over a long period requires a highly intelligent person. But does it require a certain type of mind? Most investors want to know everything—to have all the ends neatly tied off—before they make a move, but that's not possible. The investment markets are full of inconclusive evidence, and there will always be loose ends.

Lieber: I think that's absolutely right; it's a very relevant observation. I am very skeptical of people who know everything. One of the biggest investment bombs I ever saw was a friend who believed all you had to do was pick the 10 best companies in the United States and make that your portfolio.

Brouwer: How did he do?

Lieber: For a period of five or six years he was one of the most popular investment managers in the country, and then it blew up totally. He put all of his eggs in 10 great companies, but the managements of all of those companies—without exception—landed on their butts.

Brouwer: Brutal. By concentrating all his assets in a few companies, he—actually his clients—got hammered.

Lieber: Exactly. That's why we believe in broad diversification.

Brouwer: What about politics? Obviously, political trends at home and abroad impact our markets. But just how much?

Lieber: Politics is critical. We think one of the major areas you can get a huge profit from is when the rules change. For example, when Reagan came in, we decided takeovers would speed up because the government would allow any company to be bought.

Brouwer: That strategy certainly worked out well in the last two years. What's the single most important factor that moves the markets?

Lieber: As to the general price level, it is a function of fear and optimism. The biggest factor that fuels fear and greed is politics—what the overall political situation is going to be. You see, I'm very confident that it is politics that makes economic attitudes.

Brouwer: Can you explain that further?

Lieber: We live in a world of expectations. We're looking at future returns. And if you think the budget deficit is going to be successfully handled, you'll price stocks considerably higher than if you feel the deficit is going to bring about much higher inflation.

Eminently reasonable; and if you're looking at mutual

funds, that's what you want—good sense and intelligence. Steve Lieber has found long-term success with two mutual funds, and he's working on more. He knows he has to stick with the methods that made him successful in the first place.

Lieber thinks you should be skeptical, particularly of people who claim to know everything. Eliminate ego from the sell decision. And follow politics closely, because political trends rule investments.

Lieber's philosophy works very well, and it's no coincidence he has one of the most successful track records around. Take a cue from him, and do your own careful research and intelligent planning. And remember, like most valuable things in our world, investment success requires hard work. That's true even if you only have an hour a week. Make it count.

INTERVIEW: JACK LEYLEGIAN

Jack Leylegian is the president of Leylegian Investment Management, an investment advisory firm managing $300 million for retirement plans and wealthy individuals. Leylegian's portfolio management career goes back to 1967, when he started managing bond portfolios for The Northern Trust Company in Chicago.

Leylegian gained prominence in 1971 when he was hired to run the Dreyfus Fund, the flagship mutual fund of the Dreyfus Group in New York City. Just three years later he was promoted to president and chief executive officer of Dreyfus Management Inc., the giant fund family with its symbol of the lion prowling the streets and subways of Manhattan.

But Leylegian the family man wanted something more than the New York City pressure cooker. He loaded the family wagon in 1977 and moved west to San Francisco, to take charge of Bank of America's $14 billion investment management subsidiary. Four years later, Leylegian, dreaming of building a business where his family could work together, bit the bullet and started his own firm to focus more on investment management and to escape the big bank bureaucracy.

Brouwer: Let's talk about Dreyfus. How did you go to work for the Dreyfus Fund?

Leylegian: Howard Stein, the chairman, called me. He wanted to get some new blood in the management process.

Brouwer: How did he know you?

Leylegian: He checked around Wall Street and found me at The Northern Trust Company in Chicago. Howard needed a portfolio manager with experience managing billions, someone with a good track record, who understood bonds as well as stocks. And he needed a guy with experience in foreign investments, because Dreyfus was the largest domestic investor in overseas stocks and bonds.

Brouwer: What's it like to walk in each morning knowing you have billions on the line?

Leylegian: First of all, you can't react to each swing in the market. The market does its thing, and a fund that big mainly has to go along for the ride. We always tried to be in the right industry groups. But we had to be there ahead of time—when news hits in the morning, it's too late to do anything.

Brouwer: And that's probably true for the ordinary investor too, I would think.

Leylegian: The ordinary person will be at least half a day or a day behind the news. If the news items break, then the trading desks—which is really what mutual funds are—get the information instantaneously, whereas the small investor is going to hear it on the six o'clock news or the noontime report or read it in the next day's paper.

Brouwer: How do you spot trends in the market or interest rates? And how do you know when you see a trend versus a move that won't last?

Leylegian: Interest rates will determine what happens to the stock market, the bond market, and the world economy. If you just want to focus on one item, short-term interest rates are a good single indicator of where the world is going.

Brouwer: What clues do you use to spot the trend? How do you know what's a significant move?

Leylegian: What you're really looking for is not the day-to-day or week-to-week fluctuation, but a steady movement up or down.

Brouwer: How do these rates impact the economy?

Leylegian: The economy follows a normal path, except that the time it spends in each phase is not uniform. We come out of a recession because of war or because the federal government reduces interest rates. People who were afraid to borrow at 14 percent are perfectly happy to borrow at 7 or 6.

Brouwer: As a guy with many years of experience, you know how to analyze the economy, but do you think the ordinary investor has the time and knowledge to follow these trends?

Leylegian: No. Few people are going to spend the 8 to 12 hours a day that is required to gather and understand the information, just for openers. Also, most investors are emotional. When you tell investors to buy low and sell high, everybody nods their head. But when prices are low, things look bleak and unattractive—it's like asking someone to walk into a dark cave. But the top investment pro buys in when things look darkest. And then the reverse is equally true. When people read that the market is making new highs, they get caught up in the excitement, thinking it's never going to end. But it does.

Brouwer: I've felt that when the dividend yield of the S & P 500 goes substantially under three percent, that's a red flag. Do you agree with that?

Leylegian: Yes. It's important to watch the yield on the indexes. Going back 50 or 60 years, anyone can see that when the yield on the indexes sank below three percent or a little less, the market often fell out of bed.

Brouwer: That's what happened before the crash in 1973 and 1974 and now, of course, the big crash of 1987, isn't it?

Leylegian: That's right. Until this year's crash, the biggest debacle other than the Great Depression was in the 1973–74 period with the so-called Nifty Fifty stocks— IBM, Avon, Dow Chemical. They were the 50 largest stocks in the market, and they surged to unheard-of heights because people fell in love with these companies. *Everyone* agreed they were going to go up forever.

Brouwer: About the time everyone agrees on something, then the party is over. But let's get back to mutual funds. What are the basic functions of a mutual fund's portfolio manager?

Leylegian: Because the basic investment objectives of a particular fund are mandated to him, he has less freedom than most people imagine. If it's a growth stock fund, the prospectus will say the manager can only invest in growth stocks. And, in fact, he may be limited to how much cash he can raise if he sees a bad market coming. So if the mandate is growth, then the fund is going to be fully invested in growth stocks all of the time. And if the market should get hit, he's going to do substantially worse than the market.

Brouwer: How does a mutual fund family start a new mutual fund?

Leylegian: They watch what's going on, and if a particular market segment does well, they start a fund to take advantage of it. In 1974 Dreyfus started the Liquid Assets Fund—one of the first money market funds—and it went from zero to nearly $1 billion in one year. This was a time when the Dreyfus Fund's assets had been shrinking steadily, but by starting the Liquid Assets Fund, the firm's directors brought in a billion dollars almost overnight.

Brouwer: How come it grew so quickly? That was before the big spike in interest rates in the early 1980s.

Leylegian: That's exactly what the directors used to ask themselves. They spent half the board meetings fretting about whether or not this would last. Was the $1 billion a permanent asset or just a fast-growing, quick-to-fizzle fad.

Brouwer: Obviously it wasn't.

Leylegian: That's right. At the time, I was all for it. I thought to myself, we're finally giving the customer something he can't do for himself at a reasonable cost. In those days, the average person could not go out and buy a certificate of deposit because they didn't have $100,000. And even if they had $100,000, the rate was lower than it was on a $1 million certificate. We were providing a service for someone like my or your mother—someone with $20,000, who couldn't qualify for a certificate of deposit anywhere. With the money market fund, she could get higher rates, and that's why it was so successful.

Brouwer: They found out what their customers needed and gave it to them. It was a huge success and mutual fund marketing departments played it for all it was worth.

Leylegian: The mutual fund industry has never been a shrinking violet in terms of advertising. The power of advertising is awesome. Look at the millions Fidelity or Dreyfus or Franklin spend annually, it just boggles my mind.

Brouwer: The power of advertising is one reason so many people still buy high-commission load funds.

Leylegian: Mutual funds, like other investments, are sold, not bought. If the funds make it attractive enough— either with a full page ad in the *Wall Street Journal* or with incentives to a broker—people buy in.

Brouwer: How do they make it attractive?

Leylegian: They make it attractive by talking up the fund's performance. The bond funds were sold to investors who saw they could get 11 percent (as long as interest rates keep going down) when banks were only paying 7 percent. Unfortunately, that 11 percent turns out to be an illusion when rates surge back up. Sure they receive the interest, but the value of their investment in the fund sinks as interest rates rise. [This is a function of interest rate risk. The principal amount of a bond rises or falls in inverse proportion to interest rate movements.]

Brouwer: That's why long-term bond funds are less conservative than people think. It's important to buy mutual funds that are flexible. If bonds are too expensive, they can move out of them and into stocks or cash equivalents.

Leylegian: Exactly. The investor has to be perceptive enough to make sure the mutual fund he buys has the authority and the ability to shift gears.

Brouwer: Let's talk about survival. To survive, doesn't an investor have to adopt a standard of value that transcends short-term fads?

Leylegian: Yes, but the only way you learn that is by putting your money on the line. Sometimes you're right and sometimes you're wrong—that's an ugly feeling.

Brouwer: What's an example of a fund with a good long-term record that can still do well?

Leylegian: Evergreen Fund [see interview with Stephen Lieber]. The same manager has been doing it since inception. Good track record. It's still of a size where they can continue to do well.

Brouwer: If you were investing in mutual funds, how would you go about it?

Leylegian: I think you've got to temper your expectations. Everybody wants to be with a winner. So they take whoever had the best performing fund for the last quarter or the last year.

Brouwer: It's important to go with winners, but that must be measured over a market cycle, three to five years.

Leylegian: Absolutely. Anything shorter just isn't meaningful.

Brouwer: Most investors think you have to take high risk to get a good return. Do you think those go hand and hand, or can you get higher returns with reasonable risks?

Leylegian: I think you can get higher returns with reasonable risks if you're willing to swim against the current. But that takes courage.

Brouwer: What do you mean?

Leylegian: Let's say the market is at 3,000 and it drops to 1,500. The risk has been reduced immensely, so you should buy.

Brouwer: Would you put most of your investable dollars in stocks at a low point like that?

Leylegian: Yes. You have to turn your instincts on their head. When the market's at 3,000 I'll bet we're going to hear the commentators saying this is just a way station on the road to 5,000.

Brouwer: Let's talk about that. What are people going to be talking about? Let's say the market is at 3,000 or 3,600. What are they going to be saying?

Leylegian: They're going to be playing arithmetic gymnastics. Finding new ways to value the market higher and higher. People will say, since Japan sold at 60 or 70 times earnings, ours will too. New formulas will come out—it's okay to buy a stock at two times its sales or three times its book value or nine times something else.

Brouwer: People will do the equivalent of shooting an arrow and then painting a bull's eye around it.

Leylegian: Sure. And you don't have to go back very far to see this type of thing in action. Just go back to 1971–72, when the Nifty Fifty stocks were selling at 60 and 70 times earnings.

Brouwer: Will there be any safe harbors at that time?

Leylegian: Sometimes nothing works except holding on to what you have. In 1974 interest rates started to come down, but the rate of interest that you could get on a 90-day Treasury bill was still less than the rate of inflation. The stock market was heading south. So were bonds. There was no place to hide.

Leylegian believes the direction of interest rates (up or down) will determine what happens to stocks, bonds, and the economy. As an investor, you can check this out by following Treasury bill rates. Also, everyone knows you should buy low and sell high, but at the bottom of a market things look bleak and unattractive. The key is to buy when things look darkest. And, though it's been said before, it's still true: The only way to learn is to put your money on the line. Leylegian has been successfully doing just that for over 30 years.

INTERVIEW: CLAUDE ROSENBERG, JR.

Claude Rosenberg's not a flashy guy, and quite frankly, he doesn't need to be. Nor does he need to work for a living. Claude is the founder of RCM Capital Management, a San Francisco–based firm managing over $14 billion for corporate pension and profit-sharing plans, public retirement plans, foundations, and endowment funds. He later sold part of his interest in RCM to Primerica Corporation (formerly, American Can Corporation) for millions.

Rosenberg is also one of the founders of the Rosenberg Real Estate Equity Fund, generally called RREEF, the nation's fourth-largest real estate investment management firm. In addition, Rosenberg has taken his own advice over the years and built a large, well-diversified portfolio of stocks, bonds, real estate, and cash equivalents.

If that isn't enough, Rosenberg is a prolific author. His most recent book, *Investing with the Best,* is for investors who want to do a better job of selecting and tracking investment managers. In addition, he has published three other books: *The Stock Market Primer, The Common Sense Way to Stock Market Profits,* and *Psycho-Cybernetics and the Stock Market.*

Rosenberg's investment style has always been growth. Early in his 34-year investment career, he adopted a theory of investing in companies whose earnings are surging forward. He has always searched for, and found, the entrepreneurial company, the one with superior prospects of rapidly compounding growth.

Brouwer: In your book *Investing with the Best,* it sounded like you were frustrated with the investment management business. You point out the fact that there are some disreputable people whose actions demean what your firm and other reputable firms do. Is that a good read of your feelings?

Rosenberg: I think there is a frustration for anyone who is in this business. There are all kinds of games that are played, and nobody's really doing anything about it.

Brouwer: Do you think the Securities and Exchange Commission will step in with stricter rules on advertising, particularly in regard to performance claims and track records?

Rosenberg: Something will probably be done, but it is not practical to expect the authorities to devote much time to enforcement in this area. They have a lot of more pressing problems right now. So you have to take care of yourself. In other words, if you're going to entrust money to others, Buyer beware.

Brouwer: Are you saying that, in spite of all the marketing hype from investment firms, people aren't getting the objectivity and professionalism they're paying for?

Rosenberg: That's correct. Of course, people can also be their own worst enemies. They have only themselves to blame in many cases. I hope people become more contrarian, more willing to go against the grain and think for themselves. Also more skeptical of promises and performance statistics. I can't overstress the importance of avoiding the latest hot investment, and focusing on areas that are out of favor. Attention to these two points could probably make you a 50 percent better investor, all by itself.

Brouwer: Can you be more specific?

Rosenberg: First, avoid the obvious. With mutual funds, you should periodically take money from the best-performing fund, and put it in a well-run fund that's been out of favor.

Brouwer: Take money away from the best fund? Most people would think that's crazy.

Rosenberg: And difficult to do. But if you understand market cycles, you'll realize the things that worked well for the past few years will probably not work well for the next few years. The reason people seldom invest correctly is they won't make difficult decisions like this.

Brouwer: You mean bail out of a mutual fund that's hot and move into one that's been running cold?

Rosenberg: Yes. Take a fund that's not doing so well. If the fund's portfolio manager is a pro, the disappointing performance is probably due to his investment style being temporarily out of favor. For example, over-the-counter stocks have lagged the S & P 500 for a few years. Because of this underperformance, mutual funds that invest in small company stocks offer unusual value. But to take advantage of this, you have to have enough courage and self-confidence to be a contrarian.

Brouwer: What is one of the biggest or most common errors investors make?

Rosenberg: I think one of the biggest errors is assuming the future will look like the immediate past. It doesn't. Things change.

Brouwer: Investments move up or down in broad, sweeping, even cyclical movements—not a straight line from the past through the present and into the future.

Rosenberg: It's not a straight line at all. It's just the opposite.

Brouwer: How should an investor factor in risk versus the desire for top performance?

Rosenberg: People should ask what's more important, making the maximum upside or protecting yourself most on the downside. And they must realize the decision-making process is never going to be a totally clear picture.

Brouwer: Particularly in bad markets, right? In a good market, investors blithely say they can handle risk. Then, when they're down 20 or 30 percent, they panic. All of a sudden, greed is forgotten and investors berate themselves for being so aggressive.

Rosenberg: That's right. Once an investor knows his or her tolerance for risk, they also know how much they want to hedge.

Brouwer: What do you mean?

Rosenberg: If you want lower risk, you have to hedge your bets. Put less in mutual funds that buy stocks and more in money market funds or bond funds. Therefore, the investor must first identify his or her risk tolerances. Then a decision can be made, taking into account current economic and market conditions.

Brouwer: Let's move to something else you said in your book. You made the statement that for investors with less than $250,000, they should put their money in no-load mutual funds.

Rosenberg: Yes that's true, but actually the amount should be higher than that.

Brouwer: How much?

Rosenberg: Even people with millions to invest often would be better off with mutual funds. But the critical factor is not the amount of money; it's how you go about finding good funds. I think that someone has to give investors guidance on asset mix and selection of funds. A major part of my last book was devoted to helping people understand investment styles. I hoped to give people confidence that they can become an informed contrarian investor. But most people are going to need somebody else to help them to do that.

Brouwer: You're not suggesting it's a problem of intellectual capability; you just don't think most people will put in the time necessary to do what you're suggesting.

Rosenberg: That's the problem. But more importantly, I think that's the justification for your business. And provided the cost is not overwhelming, chances are your clients will do substantially better than others.

Brouwer: We talked about how people expect the future to look like the immediate past. What's another common mistake investors make?

Rosenberg: The intense interest in short-term market movements. My bias is that even though there are trading possibilities from time to time, I really wonder whether it's worth it.

Brouwer: You have said performance numbers have almost zero predictive value. Why do you think performance numbers are of so little value?

Rosenberg: Because the future will seldom look like the immediate past.

Brouwer: How is someone supposed to pick a mutual fund if they don't rely entirely on numbers?

Rosenberg: It's not that numbers are unimportant, because they do tell you how well the fund's management has performed. But you can't simply assume someone's a genius because he or she had good numbers. Nor can you assume a fund will do well in the future just because it did so in the past. It may just have been that the investment style the fund uses may have worked well for that particular market cycle.

Brouwer: How big a factor is plain luck in investment performance?

Rosenberg: It's very important. For example, when I first entered the investment business in 1955, no one dreamed that we were entering a long period of sustained economic growth that would last until 1972. In effect, this was a gift. Even though we foresaw growth at that time, neither I, nor anyone else I knew, imagined that stocks we were buying at P/Es of 8 or 10 times earnings would go to 50 or 60 times earnings.

Brouwer: And when that happened people assumed it would last forever. This was an example where people bought a simple concept—the market will slowly and certainly move ever higher. Why do people put so much faith in the latest investment fads?

Rosenberg: Because, as human beings, we are looking for simple solutions. People look for gurus. And there aren't that many investors who really want to take the time to penetrate and knock down a theory. Therefore, the quick fix solution seems good enough for them, and that's a mistake. Investment success over a long period of time is difficult.

Brouwer: What would you say if you were talking to someone who is working and planning for retirement 15 or 20 or 30 years from now?

Rosenberg: First, you have to assume responsibility for setting realistic goals and objectives. Second, you have to diversify to some degree.

Brouwer: Would it be a mistake for conservative investors to put all their money in a money market fund or CDs at a savings and loan or bank?

Rosenberg: Absolutely. Though we live in a fragile economic system, it makes sense to use several mutual funds that invest in a balanced mixture of stocks, bonds, cash equivalents, and, possibly, real estate. With this mix, you will do well under most conditions.

Brouwer: This is the approach you use for your personal investments, isn't it?

Rosenberg: Exactly. I've done this for myself as an individual. In addition to stocks and real estate, I have some of my assets in Treasury bonds and some in Treasury bills, and I don't care what I miss on the upside for that portion of my investments. But I have had to discipline myself not to look back.

Brouwer: That's very hard to do. What you're saying is that you have to be balanced, but you also have to participate in the stock market to some extent—no matter how conservative you are. Because when the market takes off, they don't ring a bell and give you time to jump on board.

Rosenberg: Right. A balanced portfolio would give you smoother investment returns. And you have to be aware that due to the interdependence of world economies, volatility and instability will not really go away completely.

Brouwer: So be prepared for periodic stormy seas.

Rosenberg: Yes. And market psychology will be increasingly important. The best investment moves are based on an analysis of the emotional attitudes, the frenzies that are occurring. If people become euphoric about the stock market as the only place to be, then serious trouble is ahead. You're going to need real guts, fortitude, to go against the flow and sell when that happens.

Brouwer: To step back into the slow lane while everyone is racing on past.

Rosenberg: And that's where your asset mix changes will have to be made to protect yourself. The more I'm in this business, the more I realize that simply getting a feel for people's enthusiasm for things is as important as anything you can do.

Brouwer: So if people see a major magazine cover with a huge arrow showing the stock market going straight up, then that's the end.

Rosenberg: That's it.

Brouwer: What's an example of this crowd mania from the recent past?

Rosenberg: Examples are everywhere. Obviously, the 508-point market panic was one example where people overdid things in a negative way. Another example is real estate. People were totally convinced by 1980 that inflation was here permanently and real estate was the only way to go. So new construction skyrocketed. For the past several years, that overbuilding snuffed out real estate growth, and in areas like Denver and Houston, overbuilding has caused serious problems.

Brouwer: Should an investor sell all stock mutual funds when the market is near a peak, or do you recommend simply reducing the amount in growth or growth and income mutual funds?

Rosenberg: Although I believe in protecting portfolio gains, I'm not a fan of the extreme form of market timing. Thus, I don't recommend being totally out of the market.

Rosenberg has consistently built wealth for his clients and himself through stock market investments over the past 34 years. But he also believes in using a balance of stocks, bonds, real estate, and cash equivalents to counteract the risk of either high inflation *or* deep deflation. He has also diversified his own assets in all of these investment categories.

He believes mutual funds are the best investment vehicle for most investors. Buy into a balanced portfolio of funds that invest in stocks, bonds, and cash equivalents—maybe real estate too.

Rosenberg is a contrarian, and he thinks investors could do much better if they avoided the latest hot investment and concentrated on out-of-favor areas. Investments that worked well for the past few years will probably not work in the next few years. Never assume the future will look like the immediate past; it doesn't. And with all your investments, remember the Roman motto—let the buyer beware.

Claude Rosenberg says stocks are the vehicle he counts on for growth in the future, for his clients and himself. Make sure you give growth a chance in your mutual fund portfolio.

INTERVIEW: MARIO GABELLI

Mario Gabelli is both an analytical number cruncher and a visionary with a telescope trained on a variety of industry horizons. When he talks about his favorite business sector—say, telecommunications companies—his eyes shine and he breaks into a spontaneous briefing on all the profitable opportunities to be seized.

But he can also spot storm clouds quickly, and he insists he won't invest in a phone company—or any company—with unproven or chancy growth prospects. He doesn't want a bet, just a sure thing. Unless he can buy in for free. That's the stubborn, hard-nosed side of his personality.

The 47-year-old Bronx native knows the value of a dollar, and this discipline keeps his optimistic, visionary side in check. His financial prudence—managing other people's money as if it were his own—can be seen in the offices of Gabelli & Company. You don't find opulent private offices with walnut paneling and marble fireplaces. No breathtaking 60th floor views.

Instead, you'll find him at his desk in a 14th floor mid-town Manhattan office, engulfed by stacks of annual reports and computer printouts. Every day, he pores over the computer spreadsheets and financial summaries churned out hourly by his earnest young research analysts.

Gabelli loves the research—the hunt for exceptional value. And this enthusiasm helps make him a top-performing mutual fund portfolio manager.

His performance speaks for itself. The Gabelli Asset Fund has averaged 22.6 percent per year since inception nearly four years ago, compared to 16 percent per year for the S & P 500. His other vehicle, GAMCO Investors—which manages money for pension plans, institutions, and individuals—has averaged 24 percent per year for the past 12 years. His firm also manages Gabelli Equity Trust (closed-end fund) plus three other mutual funds: Gabelli Growth, Gabelli Value, and Gabelli Convertible.

When he opened his firm in 1977, Mario Gabelli struggled to attract clients. Managing a few million dollars seemed like a big deal back then. How things have changed. Recently, Shearson Lehman Hutton raised nearly $1.2 billion (yes, billion) for Gabelli Value, his latest fund. Overall, the firm manages over $6.5 billion.

Through it all, Gabelli's style hasn't changed very much. It still boils down to one essential: the quest for undervalued stocks. He lives, eats, and breathes the stock market. He loves rapidly growing stocks, but he doesn't like to bet on unproven growth—unless he can buy it for free. Getting growth for free may seem unlikely, but in the interview you will find out how he got free growth in one of the hottest deals of the 1980s. And you'll also find out the industry he thinks will do the same for the 1990s.

Brouwer: How did you get started looking for undervalued stocks?

Gabelli: I started out in the investment business as an analyst covering several industries: auto parts, farm equipment, durable goods. I looked at cyclical companies, growth companies. Like any analysts, our job was to gather the data, do the analysis. But the tricky part was to understand what a business—the whole company—was worth. This was in the late 60s. A few years later, I watched companies get ravaged by high inflation. We had the first oil shock. Bloated inventories.

Brouwer: Pretty depressing time for stocks.

Gabelli: Yes, people were wondering why they should own stocks at all. In 1977, I started Gabelli & Co. to get back to basics. My goal was to focus on what I thought to be the most fundamental element. We looked at stocks as a share of a business. You only buy the stock because the business makes sense to own. From that you could decide what the business was worth and from that, what one share was worth.

Brouwer: What type of businesses do you look for?

Gabelli: Because I was an auto parts analyst, I understood early on what was going on with Japanese businesses. At that time, I made the decision not to buy businesses that compete directly with the Japanese.

Brouwer: Good move. What else?

Gabelli: I also wanted companies that could adjust pricing as inflation accelerated. Another important requirement was predictable, steadily growing earnings.

Brouwer: So you're looking for undervalued companies that have growth potential?

Gabelli: I like to buy a business at a big discount from what it's worth. And I take a long-term outlook. If I buy something today, I know I am going to sell it in 5 to 10 years.

Brouwer: Why 5 to 10 years?

Gabelli: That's how long it takes to make real money. Even in cable television or the cellular telephone industries, it took a long time before investors made any money in it. For a business to take shape and develop, given the particular dynamics of its industry, you need time, lots of time.

Brouwer: You did extremely well in the cellular telephone stocks. And you saw that trend before most investors. How did you decide to buy in? How did you see the growth potential so early on?

Gabelli: Let me tell you a story that illustrates my philosophy on growth. I was asked to serve on the committee to honor Columbus and his discovery of the New World. I told them, "Terrific, but you've got the wrong guy." I would never have financed Columbus. I wouldn't have doubted his theory that the world was round. I just didn't think he could make any money on his first trip. I'm not a venture capitalist. I won't buy a new idea just because someone thinks it will be good; I only buy what is already good. Unless I can get it for free.

Brouwer: How do you get it for free?

Gabelli: We began investing in Lin Broadcasting about 20 years ago. We revisited the company just at the time they were beginning to file applications for cellular franchises. They owned a number of broadcasting properties and the stock was so cheap you could get their basic broadcasting business for 60 cents on the dollar, with the cellular play thrown in for free.

Brouwer: That's obviously quite different from investing in a startup situation in the hopes the technology does what it's supposed to do, isn't it?

Gabelli: Yes, we weren't willing to bet on the next generation of semiconductors or the hottest new computer workstation. That we never wanted to do.

Brouwer: Why was the cellular business so attractive, besides the fact you got into it for free?

Gabelli: Well, I was following cable television companies and I knew what a franchise was worth per subscriber, or even per house the cable passed by. I knew how to evaluate that. Plus, I had always had a CB radio and I was very sensitive to the fact that a person in a car would love to be able to communicate. With cellular, everything came together. You had something people want—the ability to communicate from their car—and the technology was already in place. Everyone knows how to use a telephone. Once the FCC awarded franchises, that was it; everything fell in place.

Brouwer: Going beyond cellular, why are you so excited about ordinary telephone companies?

Gabelli: We are buying businesses that over the next 5 to 10 years will create enormous wealth the same way cable television properties did over the past 10 years.

Brouwer: That sounds like you anticipate rapid growth.

Gabelli: Going back to the notion of value investing versus growth investing, when we analyze a business, we love to have growth. But we are not looking for a new widget. We'll take an industry that's existing, but previously looked kind of dull. That way we can buy in at a big discount. This is one of the industries you dream about. Major, major technological revolution taking place. Right now the telephone industry can give you voice messages, but soon fiber optics will expand that dramatically.

Brouwer: Why is that?

Gabelli: Fiber optics technology is like a 100-lane highway going to your home compared to the present system of a twisted-pair copper wire, which is the equivalent of a two-lane country road.

Brouwer: The perfect growth opportunity.

Gabelli: Right. The telephone companies are providing new services and those are driving demand up. For instance, something simple like an answering machine. Before, the phone would just ring; now you get a message and the phone company generates revenue because your caller got through. Plus, the industry is being deregulated. That will also allow growth.

Brouwer: Given what's happened with other "deregulated" industries, that doesn't sound that exciting.

Gabelli: But it is. It is becoming apparent that the United States can't win an economic war against Japan and/or

Germany by having major industries, like telephone, tied to the "cost plus" system of utility rate-of-return regulation. And on March 16, 1989, the Federal Communications Commission said they were moving ahead with plans to deregulate.

Brouwer: This is an example of how you look ahead to get dramatic capital appreciation without betting on new, unproven technology. Do you really think telephone companies are the next big investment opportunity.

Gabelli: It's one we see very clearly. Primarily, the independent telephone companies, as opposed to those that were spun off from Ma Bell five years ago.

Brouwer: Going beyond this area, we all know there are cycles in investing. Will there be a point where so many people are looking for these undervalued situations that they dry up?

Gabelli: There will be periods where our returns won't look as good as others. I am convinced we are going to do well, but not always on a relative basis. But what distinguishes us is that we don't care about the Standard & Poor's 500 Index. Many people do, but we don't. We are investing our clients' money as though it were our own.

Brouwer: What is your personal benchmark for performance?

Gabelli: We want to earn 10 percent, after taxes and after inflation.

Brouwer: That's quite a goal.

Gabelli: Now we don't know how long we are going to be able to do that. Consider the island of Manhattan. The Dutch bought it for $24 in 1626. Today it's worth $30 trillion. That seems like a phenomenal return, but it's only eight percent per year with no adjustment for inflation or taxes. So 10 percent after inflation and taxes is a big hurdle to clear.

Brouwer: Why not compare yourself to the S & P 500?

Gabelli: Because you always have the alternative not to be in stocks at all. We have to consider what we do compared to a virtually risk-free investment such as Treasury bills. And, of course, if you want to build wealth you have to consider taxes and inflation.

Brouwer: What about mistakes? Have you made many, and how do you deal with them when you do?

Gabelli: We make all types of mistakes. We don't buy stocks that subsequently go up. We buy stocks that don't do anything, and we buy ones that go down. We sometimes buy a stock because we think some corporate event is going to enhance value. For example, Curtiss-Wright. We bought it several years ago at $35. The chairman was in his early 70s and another company, Teledyne, owned 56 percent of Curtiss-Wright. We thought Teledyne would buy the balance. They didn't. Then Curtiss-Wright went out and lost $100 million on Western Union. So we've owned the stock for years and, from our point of view, it hasn't been a success.

Another example. About 12 years ago we started looking at Mississippi river barges used to ship agricultural products—for example, corn. Barges have a cost advantage over rail and there is no possibility of obsolescence because the locks on the river can't be changed in size. We analyzed all the factors and they looked great. What we didn't factor in was a presidential embargo of food grain exports to Russia after the Soviet invasion of Afghanistan.

In other words, we can, and have, been blindsided by major policy changes. We talked a lot about the growth potential for independent telephone companies. The risk there is, first, that the trend towards deregulation gets derailed and, second, that inflation accelerates.

Brouwer: Let's go back to investor basics. Why do you think the public is so fascinated by market timing?

Gabelli: It goes back to when I was growing up in the 50s. The word then was that smart guys always put a stop loss order [a stop loss order is an order to sell a stock if it drops to a pre-determined level]. If the stock goes down by 10 percent, your sell order goes into effect. What happened on October 19, 1987 was a massive wave of stop loss selling by the big guys, the big institutions.

These institutions often think of stocks, not as ownership of a business, but as financial instruments designed to be traded to generate profits. Today, you have an environment where instant gratification is important and where stocks have become, in effect, mere commodities. Even sophisticated investors who should know better get caught up in this.

Brouwer: Can you give me an example?

Gabelli: I had a guy, one of our large clients, come in here shortly after the 190-point market drop on October 13, 1989. And he came in and said he wanted everything sold—all the stocks. I told him he had said the same thing after the crash in 1987. We kept him in back then and his account was up dramatically. Yet all he could think of was he wanted to sell. Had nothing to do with anything logical. It was just the market was down nearly 200 points. So you have a historical record of hysterical reactions to the ups and downs.

Brouwer: A historical record of hysteria. That's not bad, Mario. What do you think is a better way?

Gabelli: My cult is buy when things are down and sell when they go up.

Brouwer: I didn't know you had a cult.

Gabelli: It's a cult. The Gabelli cult.

Brouwer: You have worked at several different brokerage firms before starting your own firm. Can people get good information and objective advice from the major brokerage firms?

Gabelli: Yes . . . maybe. The problem is that good brokers understand that their book of business depends entirely on the loyalty of their customers. Unfortunately, the young guys who dial for dollars are often on what Wall Street calls a "search and destroy mission." You search for customers and if you destroy them, you just search for new ones.

Brouwer: What do you think is a better system?

Gabelli: Brokers are subject to a lot of internal pressures. If he doesn't generate enough revenue, his chair is given to someone else. And so you have a problem.

Brouwer: As an alternative, do you think people can do well if they simply invest in a portfolio of quality no-load mutual funds. No in-and-out trading, just long-term buy and hold?

Gabelli: I think your approach to finding the highest quality no-loads makes a lot of sense. And it goes in the client's best interest. So you are at the cutting edge of where the Street should be. You know and I know it.

Brouwer: To get back to invest practices in your mutual funds. There are times—such as the present—when you build up a lot of cash. You receive money from takeover deals, new investors come in. How do you handle this?

Gabelli: I need a good old-fashioned market panic.

Brouwer: You're hoping for a panic?

Gabelli: Well, I'm not hoping for a panic, but I need a down market—a time when negative emotions are running high—for an extended period. Years ago, market corrections would last for months. And they gave us time to get cash invested. Now it might last a day or even a few hours. You just don't have time to build a position.

Brouwer: Speaking of time, how about you? You now have several mutual funds plus your separately managed accounts—over $6.5 billion all together. Are you running out of time?

Gabelli: From the point of view of 21 years ago when I joined Loeb Rhodes as a rookie analyst, I used to spend 50 percent of my time doing research and 50 percent communicating those ideas to our clients. Today, I am still spending only 50 percent of my time doing research and 50 percent having board meetings, writing letters, meeting clients.

There are some advantages, though. Ten years ago I had to go visit many companies, where today some of them come see me. I have analysts to do much of the legwork that I did before. However, I used to go and see 50 to 100 new companies each year. Today, I'm probably only seeing 50 to 75. I'm losing something there, and that could hurt over the next 10 years.

Brouwer: Is it more, or less, fun now?

Gabelli: (Long pause.) I would say it is more of a problem now because of the expectations of people who have entrusted money to us. They are demanding returns that are not sustainable.

Brouwer: That could be dangerous.

Gabelli: Exactly. We had the dean of a major college come to see us, asking us to put more of their endowment fund assets into stocks rather than, say, Treasury bills. Basically, they have done better than their wildest dreams because he had the courage to invest in stocks during the 80s bull market. But we had to tell him that for the university's sake the asset mix should be toned down to have less stocks. We don't like to be mentors. We are investors. But we find ourselves cast in the role of being the anchor to misguided enthusiasm.

Brouwer: On the other hand, when stocks have done badly, when everything is gloomy, you have to convince people like that to be optimistic about stocks.

Gabelli: That we don't mind doing. We've always done that.

Brouwer: Can you happily continue running the firm for 20 or 30 years?

Gabelli: I love to look at stocks and I will always love it. Do I want to run the administrative side of several mutual funds. No. Absolutely not. I don't see doing that for 20 years. For example, the amount of paperwork you have to do just to buy a big position in a small company stock will really start wearing us out. Money managers are being stuck with layers and layers of bureaucracy.

Brouwer: What are you going to do?

Gabelli: Well, Peter Lynch had one of the best jobs in the business. He got to spend all of his day analyzing stocks with very little administrative stuff to distract him. One other problem is that I own more that 50 percent of my firm. I get all the credit when things go right, all the blame when they go wrong. But the responsibility of an error is so Draconian. If I am out for two, three days a week doing research, it's a potential time bomb. Any one of the 100 staff members could say something—even something well-intentioned—that would come back to haunt me for failure to supervise properly. We've made sure we have the best procedures in place and we have people to monitor our compliance with these procedures. But still I worry.

Brouwer: Why so many regulations?

Gabelli: We are in an environment where people are reacting strongly to real scoundrels like Ivan Boesky. Everyone in the investment business is being tainted by those few.

Brouwer: What's next for you?

Gabelli: Managing money is fun. Finding great stocks is fun. And it has to be kept that way. I want to do this for another 30 years, maybe more. My goal is the year 2020. But to do that we have to change. To get rid of the negatives.

Brouwer: Would you perhaps go public? Sell enough to get your ownership under 50 percent?

Gabelli: No. But we want to gain more exposure to international markets. So having a well-heeled foreign partner with access, not just to money, but to good international stocks would be of interest. We are not there yet though.

A high return after taxes and inflation is Mario Gabelli's goal, and it should be yours, too. Inflation takes a bite out of the purchasing power of your assets every single day. Whether it's two percent, six percent or 10, you have to plan for it. Getting growth for free is one way to do it.

Gabelli does his own research and you should too. He knows that reliance on the vagaries of Wall Street's advice guarantees mediocrity.

Do your own research, make your own decisions, invest in

a portfolio of quality no-load mutual funds. If you do you will, as Gabelli pointed out, "be at the cutting edge of where the Street should be."

INTERVIEW: ROY NEUBERGER

Interviewing Roy Neuberger reminded me of talking with my grandfather. Before I settled in the chair, he started peppering me with questions. I instinctively wanted to bare my psyche to this cherubic, seemingly ageless man. He's a combination Delphic oracle, kindly grandfather, historian, and humanist. I knew I had lost control of the interview, so I could only buckle up and hope for the best.

Neuberger is the quintessential renaissance man. Originally, he had hoped to be a great painter, but by 1924 he faced the truth that the talent simply wasn't there. After giving it his best, Neuberger calmly assessed his progress and found it wanting. He knew he would never be the genius he had hoped to become. Instead of being embittered, Neuberger the artist became Neuberger the collector.

His father had died in 1916, leaving him with an inheritance that threw off enough income to live on. And live he did—in 1924, he moved to Paris and spent four years on the Left Bank, studying, collecting art, and savoring the cafes near his small apartment on the Boulevard St. Germain. The twenties were the golden age for the City of Lights, a lusty time filled with fabulous art, literature, and memorable people.

Neuberger practically lived in the oddly named Cafe de Deux Magots, one of several Left Bank spots immortalized in books by Ernest Hemingway. James Joyce lived just down the street, but Neuberger, consumed by his passion for art, never bothered to look him up. By chance, he met Thornton Wilder in a bookstore about the time his classic *The Bridge of San Luis Rey* came out.

In 1929, Neuberger decided he needed more money to invest in art. His modest inheritance was enough for the student life in Paris, but his passion for art seemed to know no bounds. Did the inconvenience of having very little money stop him? No. Neuberger, the collector, headed back to New York City to become a stockbroker and accumulate cash to buy the art he loved.

Although generally a man with exquisite timing, Neuberger couldn't have journeyed to Wall Street at a worse time. He arrived on March 9, 1929, just seven months before the most devastating market crash in history. But his instincts saved him. Somehow, this market neophyte decided the party was over and began to short Radio Corporation of America, the most active stock on the Big Board, just before the crash. (Shorting a stock is a way to profit when it drops in price. Investors who want to sell short actually sell stock they don't own. Their broker arranges for them to borrow shares from someone who owns the stock. At some point, the investor then has to close out the transaction and buy the stock in the open market, returning the borrowed shares. The idea, of course, is to sell at a high price and buy back much lower—the reverse of buy low, sell high.)

Neuberger didn't ride RCA all the way from its bull market high of $114 down to its 1932 low between $2 and $3, but he did sell short at $100 and profited from the slide down. This one instinctive move insured him permanent membership in the Wall Street Hall of Fame.

He went on to launch his present firm, Neuberger & Berman, in 1939, at the age of 36. Far from the largest of money management firms, Neuberger & Berman oversees $18 billion for retirement plans, trusts, individuals, and its family of no-load mutual funds. Three of the funds—Partners, Manhattan, and Guardian—regularly show up on mutual fund rankings as low-risk high-performers.

Neuberger started the first fund, Guardian, in 1950 and produced a solid record of stable growth for 28 years. The fund's average annual return was 10.76 percent, compared to 10.26 percent for Standard & Poor's 500 Index over the same period. In addition, Guardian's results were more consistent. Under Neuberger's management, Guardian Fund beat the benchmark index for a remarkable period of nearly three decades.

Neuberger's first market coup in RCA gives us an insight to his investment strategy, which is, very simply, *"Make money any way you can."* If the market's going up, go with it. If it's going down, sell short and profit on the downside. Few investors have this flexibility or courage. Fewer still manage to remain relaxed while doing it.

Perhaps it is Neuberger's original attitude. He only went into stocks to pay for his first love, art; maybe that outlet gives him the psychological distance most lack. In his eighties, Neuberger is sharp, energetic, and very entertaining. It may be his love of life or of people, or simply his enjoyment of art. Whatever his secret is, it works.

His investments in art have been just as savvy and successful as his Wall Street techniques, although he refuses to talk about art as an investment. Neuberger despises any attempt to put commercial value on artistic works. But in the thirties, stocks weren't the only investments that were cheap. The art world was just as depressed as the stock market; the big buyers were broke. Neuberger, the bargain-hunting contrarian, didn't try to buy Old Masters; he wanted American artists—people he could meet and talk to. People who shared some of the same experiences he did.

As his business prospered in the forties and fifties, he went on a buying binge that would make any present-day museum director drool. He bought works by American artists such as Milton Avery, Jackson Pollock, Willem de Kooning, Edward Hopper, Peter Hurd, and many more when their works sold for hundreds instead of hundreds of thousands. He collected so many treasures that the State University of New York had to build a museum to house the art works he gave it in 1974. Those were only a portion of his total collection. His home and the walls of Neuberger & Berman's midtown Manhattan offices are filled with his fantastic collection of vivid, colorful paintings and prints.

Brouwer: Roy, just to preserve appearances, I'll ask you the first few questions. When did you found Neuberger & Berman?

Neuberger: In 1939, but we got started in 1940.

Brouwer: How did you get started in the investment business initially?

Neuberger: Oh, I came back from living abroad as an expatriate in the twenties, and my goal was to buy the work of living artists. And I needed to have some ambition and money. Ambition was easy to come by, but money wasn't at that time. I had a fair amount of capital, but nowhere near enough to do what I wanted. So I had to go to work where I could make some real money. Where do you go to work? Wall Street. So I came down March 9.

Brouwer: March 9, 1929?

Neuberger: Yes. It was good for gaining experience. I had a panic on my hands within seven months.

Brouwer: Where did you start?

Neuberger: A small brokerage firm called Halle & Steiglitz. The first year I learned the business by going into every department: research, trading, the back office. At the time of the crash, I was working in what was called purchase and sales. So I saw the transactions of Papa Joe Kennedy. He was a pretty big speculator, selling stocks short. And we handled a number of other big players like him. Halle & Steiglitz was somewhere between a medium-sized and a very large brokerage firm. Good place to learn.

Brouwer: We know you made some good investments for your own account in 1929. When did you start managing money for the public?

Neuberger: I started as a broker, almost an investment counselor, in March 1930. I got paid in brokerage, regular commissions. And soon my clients gave me power of attorney to manage accounts on a discretionary basis.

Brouwer: When did you first know you had a distinct investment style or philosophy?

Neuberger: It developed from 1929 to 1930. In 1929 I only took care of my own money. In 1930 a few people said, you can do better than my broker or my investment adviser. In those days, there weren't many investment advisers, and they were mainly up in Boston. They considered themselves very high-class, but I thought they were very snooty.

Brouwer: Do you think you are still learning about investments?

Neuberger: I feel that the process of learning goes on continually as far as the market's concerned. And now it's very much complicated by the technological age.

Brouwer: How do you diagnose trends in the stock market?

Neuberger: I figure that a bull market is illogical, irrational, and you can't diagnose how far it is going to go. But it always ends. Then you have a bear market, and during that you can usually tell the bottom. The hard part is having the money to buy all the cheap stocks at that time.

Brouwer: How do you tell the bottom?

Neuberger: There's no formula, but you can tell. You know when the bottom was hit in 1929, it wasn't a real bottom. When the real bottom was reached was 1932. Then in 1937 we had a bad break in the market. The next bad collapse was 1946. And after that there wasn't a bear market until 1962. That was my very best call: 1961 and 1962. I diagnosed it and got quick action.

Brouwer: Now how did you do that?

Neuberger: I identified 700 for the Dow Jones Industrials as high and potentially dangerous. The market topped at about 735.

Brouwer: Why was 700 high? Today the Dow is much higher.

Neuberger: 700 was high because of the P/E multiples. Xerox was 77 times earnings at that time. The market or Dow Jones average P/E multiple was 22½. And new issues [initial public offerings of a corporation's shares] were selling at ridiculously high prices and there were just tons of them.

Brouwer: So what do you do at a time like that? Do you sell out completely or do you take some profits?

Neuberger: I'm going to say two seemingly contradictory things. First, a stock that is working out requires patience. Many people are so afraid it will go back down, they sell too early. But then, usually in a very strong market, when the stock in question moves beyond a reasonable valuation, you must have the courage to sell it. The same applies to the market as a whole.

Brouwer: As a believer in mutual funds, do you think the average investor needs to be concerned about the stock market?

Neuberger: Yes, in broad terms, because stocks are the underlying investment of many funds. Obviously, someone who buys stocks directly has to spend a lot more time following individual stocks and the market.

Brouwer: Do you do much economic analysis? Do you think people are overburdened with debt?

Neuberger: Yes, I do. I think the great mass of people are not in good shape. There is still a lot of unemployment, and the gap between rich and poor is increasing.

Brouwer: Of course, people who are rich, like yourself, are not about to give up what they've earned.

Neuberger: No, but it should be used productively, to build businesses that will employ people and give them good working conditions and a chance to grow.

Brouwer: You are pretty pessimistic about the future of the economy. Why do you feel that way?

Neuberger: I look to the 1990s with a lot of fear for our country and its people. We may have social problems such as we had in the Depression where lots of people—even the wealthy—became socialists. I wasn't rich enough to be a socialist then, and I paid more attention to learning my business and learning about art. But I am worried about the future.

Brouwer: So, fundamentally, we have some serious problems in our economy, both nationally and in the world. How do you translate this into action in the investment market?

Neuberger: I do a simplified form of evaluation of securities. I look at things the old-fashioned way. But I've also been a chartist, and the charts are a big help to me.

Brouwer: Do you track market movements and use that information to predict future movements in the market and in particular stocks?

Neuberger: Yes. I also look at interest rates. The trend in the market is highly dependent on the trend in interest rates. Rising interest rates indicate that the Federal Reserve believes the economy is overheating. Their prescription for cooling off the economy usually means the market is going to go from hot to frigid very soon.

Brouwer: After interest rates, what else do you watch?

Neuberger: The business cycle and the market cycle. But remember, these are different. Many people assume that since the economy is doing well, the market will also. But the market and the economy seldom go in the same direction for very long. Up markets generally last longer than down markets. Up markets often last a couple of years, while bear markets usually are short-lived though very steep declines. It's important to remain positive in bad markets and a bit cautious in good markets. Going against the grain, in effect.

Brouwer: How did you get the idea to start the Guardian fund?

Neuberger: I believed it was a sensible method for a person to invest, and I disliked the 8½ percent sales load most mutual funds charged, because I thought it was excessive. I still do. With a load fund, when you put $10,000 in a fund, after commissions you are down to $9,150. The only essential difference between a load and a no-load fund is the commission. The management can be the same people in many cases.

Brouwer: Why do you like mutual funds?

Neuberger: I think mutual funds are a way for any individual—whether he has $2,000 or $100 million—to make a sound investment.

Brouwer: What's the difference between investing in a mutual fund versus opening an account at an investment advisory firm?

Neuberger: You get very little difference, except that the adviser can tailor the account a bit to your taste. The investment adviser's fee is probably slightly higher for an individual than the same fee would be in a mutual fund. And you can find mutual funds that are made for you. For example, even though we haven't got a big empire like the others, we have several different mutual funds, each of which has different investment objectives.

Brouwer: How can a conservative investor deal with such a volatile and fragile financial system?

Neuberger: Remain cautious. Keep plenty of money in cash. Be very careful to use mutual funds that are value investors. [Value investors focus on companies with sound finances and solid business prospects. The emphasis is on companies selling at a low P/E.] And when the next crash comes, be ready to take advantage of it.

Brouwer: You've lived a well-rounded life. What do you think the key is?

Neuberger: Education is as important an element as exists, except for nature itself. Physical nature.

Brouwer: That's a pretty strong statement.

Neuberger: Our educational system has some great advantages, but most Americans aren't taking advantage of it properly. We don't have enough people studying engineering and technology. We have too many people studying law.

Brouwer: Besides education, what else is important?

Neuberger: My love of art has given me a great deal of pleasure in life.

Brouwer: Are you still buying paintings?

Neuberger: Yes, but I never bought them as an investment. I don't think I have ever sold a painting. Given many away, but never sold. Now, I still buy them because, I guess, I am a victim of habit.

Brouwer: How do you decide what to buy?

Neuberger: I always buy the same way. My formula now, more than ever, is to buy somebody you never heard of.

Brouwer: That's easy. I know very little about contemporary art.

Neuberger: In the 1950s I bought Jackson Pollock, even though at that time his works didn't seem cheap at $800.

Brouwer: How much would that be worth today?

Neuberger: I don't know, but I recently saw an insurance appraisal for a Pollock I donated to the Neuberger museum in Westchester, N.Y. The painting was appraised at $3.5 million.

Brouwer: Your third fortune was made in real estate. What do you think about real estate in general?

Neuberger: Rural land is probably the best long-term investment, if you're going to live two hundred years.

Brouwer: Great. If you're not?

Neuberger: Then for the next few years I think real estate is difficult. I believe we're going to have a crash in New York City. It's only a matter of when. New York City has been the biggest boom in the country. We're overbuilding here, and we're going to have a crash in both commercial and residential.

Brouwer: When did you buy real estate?

Neuberger: Personally, I created a partnership in 1968, when the stock market was unattractive. You were too young to have paid much attention to it then. And it was a good idea to switch from stocks to real estate.

Brouwer: How did you make that decision?

Neuberger: I felt the market was overheating. And I believe in being flexible. If stocks are too high, look around.

Brouwer: Would you buy real estate now at this point?

Neuberger: Not in New York City. I own real estate in

Chicago and St. Louis. All buildings built before 1930.
They're not as dangerous as a hotshot new project.

Brouwer: What about real estate investment trusts (REITs)
and things like that? Do you ever buy those?

Neuberger: Yes. But I wouldn't feel at home being a bull on
real estate right now.

Brouwer: How do you stay so calm? I know you walk quite
a bit for exercise. What else do you do? Tennis? Golf?

Neuberger: I used to play tennis, but I quit.

Brouwer: Why?

Neuberger: I'd be dead if I played tennis the way I used to,
because I played to win.

And win he has. In stocks and in art and in real estate.
Neuberger's record of accomplishments covers a remarkable
span of years and events. He prospered through the Great
Depression, World War II, the 1950s, the 1960s, the wild
inflationary 1970s, and the turbulent 1980s. At every twist
and tortuous turn in this 58-year period, he made money—
in stocks, bonds, and real estate—while building a superb
brokerage and money management firm that ranks among
the nation's finest.

Neuberger pointed out a false assumption people make.
They assume that since the economy is doing well, the stock
market will also. But the market and the economy seldom go
in the same direction for long.

He is a strong believer in no-load mutual funds. Whether
you have $2,000 or $100 million, mutual funds make a sound
investment.

Neuberger's career points out the value of a long-term point
of view. Many people refuse to plan for the future, thinking it's
too far away. Had Neuberger adopted that attitude, he would
not only have shortchanged himself and his family, but also
the partners and staff at Neuberger & Berman, their clients,
and the hundreds of thousands of shareholders in the firm's
mutual funds. And let's not forget the thousands who have
enjoyed his paintings on display at the Neuberger museum in
Purchase, N.Y. Think long term like Roy Neuberger and the
other investment pros. The rewards may surprise you.

11

Winning Demands Desire, Drive, and Determination

You've been drilled on chalkboard strategies, and your helmet is strapped on. You've practiced, prepared, and scrimmaged for 10 chapters. Now it's time to get out of the locker room and hit the field to put your game to the test.

Success—in sports, investments, or life itself—is earned with desire, drive, and determination. Forget good intentions. Whether on a muddy football field, in a 12-meter racing sloop, in a business office, or on a factory floor, winners succeed because they think smart, work hard and control their emotions.

For many investors the most difficult challenge will be learning to control their emotions. In Chapter 4 we explored that old saying, buy low and sell high, and you learned some objective benchmarks to help you value the stock market and determine what low and high really mean. No matter how clearly you understand these concepts intellectually, you will find it very difficult to think and act for yourself during periods of market extremes. Why? Because you're human and you have strong emotions when it comes to your money.

When the market is soaring it appears as if it could go on forever. All around you people will be raking in big profits. The market will be drawing intense media coverage and the temptation to stay in will be very strong. But if you see that the market has reached or exceeded the valuation benchmarks, you *must* take action to reduce risk. Take profits out of your funds and move that money into money market funds. Batten the hatches (see Chapter 4). Making this move will not be easy, but doing so is critical to your long-term success. Remember Baron Rothschild. You must control your greed and be willing to let someone else get those last few points.

At market valleys, fear will be tugging at your heart. Market bottoms do not occur without widespread feelings of gloom and doom. You will *not* be immune to these feelings. Don't blithely assume you will be able to control them. At the bottom, most investors simply give up. They capitulate; throw in the towel, the washcloth and even the shower curtain. The headlines will be uniformly bad. Interest rates will be high. If the market is at 1,200, the "gurus" will be looking for 900. Buying in will not be easy. But you *must* summon the courage and do it.

How can you avoid this emotional whipsaw? By having a solid game plan and sticking to it. Use the market valuation benchmarks and when they indicate a market top or bottom, take action. At time like those, the statistics are far more reliable than your, or anyone else's feelings. Human nature places far too much emphasis on recent events and we often ignore the bigger picture. When the market is running at floodtide there will be many people who find seemingly plausible reasons why it can go much higher. And when it has plunged to bear market lows, those same seers will find reasons why it should go much lower. Listening to all the current opinions theories, and wacky notions on investing would unsettle anyone's mind.

In Chapter 2, I said, "Planning your next investment move these days is like driving in the fog. Even if you manage to get home, your nerves are shot and you wonder if it was worth the aggravation." By now, you've learned exactly how to cut through the fog and invest like a pro. But knowledge alone isn't enough. How many times have you embarked on something with great enthusiasm only to lose interest? Yet in today's lighting-fast investment markets, you can lose more than interest if your attention wanders. Invest carelessly, and your assets could dwindle or even vanish.

Establish a routine, and stick to it no matter what happens. Be realistic—and disciplined. If you can only commit one hour every two weeks to your investments, that's okay. Just make sure you keep that solitary hour sacred, inviolable. Block out that time in your appointment book or calendar. Reserve those hours and keep your appointment with success. Time is limited, so keep your eye focused on your goals—and on your money.

Great investors, like top athletes, specialize. They don't try to be expert or even highly knowledgeable about every single type of investment. Instead, they concentrate their efforts on those few select areas that work for them. You should do the same. Zero in on your goals and objectives; hammer out your own personal balance of risk and reward. Write down your goals.

Make them part of your life. You are far more likely to reach your goals if you write them down and measure your personal progress. Chalk up your winners, and document your defeats.

Precious free time seems to evaporate, so you need some help sorting things out. Fortunately, you don't have to start from scratch. There is no need to devote hours to poring over the stock tables in the paper; that's the pro's job. You can invest the lion's share of your time in things you love: family, work, your home, sports, hobbies, and other activities.

If you only have an hour or two a week for your investment program, you have to specialize. There simply isn't enough time to follow the stock market, bonds, real estate, mutual funds, limited partnerships, foreign exchange, and a hundred other possible investments. Face the fact that you can't do everything. Trying to juggle a dozen balls means you're going to drop most of them, and that will hurt.

To help you navigate the riptides and reefs, shoals and sandbars, let's take a hard look at the investing do's and don'ts we've covered. Here is a quick summary of investment fundamentals, tips, quips, red flags, and green lights — bedrock concepts you should use as the foundation for building a solid, growing investment portfolio:

□ Before you do any investing, make sure you have three to six months of "rainy day" money in a bank account or money market fund and have adequate health and life insurance. Don't spend a penny on mutual funds or other investments without building a bundle of personal security.

□ Remember Brouwer's Basics for bulletproof investing:
  □ Set clear objectives and guidelines.
  □ Use investments that mirror your objectives.
  □ Coattail with the pros.
  □ Track results, cut losses, and stick with winners.

□ Invest for the long pull. Remember how people make money in real estate: They buy and hold. Let the compounding effect of solid, annual investment returns go to work for you.

□ There is so much information today, it's like trying to sip from a fire hose. Find a few sources of understandable information and forget about the rest.

□ Don't chase last year's hot mutual fund. Remember the study of top annual mutual fund performers. Last year's super star could be this year's black hole.

□ Mutual funds are the ideal investment vehicle, because they combine professional management, low minimum investments, flexibility, diversification, and a low-cost fee structure in one package. Funds offer a wide range of investment options and comfort, because they are more stringently regulated than most other investments you could consider.

□ Don't crapshoot with your cash. The best investments are profitable yet unexciting—even mundane. Look for excitement from your job, family, friends, or hobbies, not from your portfolio.

- ☐ Historically, stock mutual funds have produced growth, while bond funds and money market funds have cushioned portfolios in down trends.
- ☐ There are three kinds of risk you must watch out for:
  - ☐ Market risk.
  - ☐ Default or bankruptcy risk.
  - ☐ Sector risk.

With a portfolio of diversified mutual funds you can nearly eliminate both default or bankruptcy risk and sector risk, but market risk is always a factor. You have to develop the emotional fortitude to ride out the downturns. A solid portfolio of mutual funds can help put the brakes on market slides.

- ☐ Don't be afraid of being different—contrarian. Contrarian thinking, while often misunderstood, is the ability to swim upstream, to go against the flow. It takes nerve, brains, and a strong ego to be different. But it also takes intelligence to realize when the crowd is correct, or at least temporarily unstoppable.
- ☐ No one is immune to panics and crashes. Don't get so caught up in current events that you forget history. The market moves in broad cycles. Use the techniques in Chapter 4 to see where you are in the stock market cycle. Learn to avoid being overenthusiastic at stock market peaks and don't be depressed and deflated at the bottom.
- ☐ Short-term market timing rarely works. Don't base your strategy on trying to pick the absolute pinnacle or the deepest trough of the market. Baron Rothschild had the answer—others could have the 20 percent profits at the top and bottom, he wanted the 60 percent gain in the middle.
- ☐ Become informationally fit. To be a well-rounded investor, you need to do your own research and exercise your mind. Stick to an exercise program that is tightly focused to your personal situation.
- ☐ Use your public library. The information sources and the trained staff are amazing resources, paid for with your tax dollars. You have the right to this help; exercise it.

- □ Use the *Wiesenberger Investment Company Service* as your main prospecting tool to locate a few great mutual funds. Don't waste your time trying to become a general investment expert. Just discard the many mediocre funds and concentrate on the top ones.
- □ Once you have found funds you like, read the prospectus, statement of additional information, and quarterly reports *before* investing. Invest your time before you invest your cash.
- □ Watch out for mutual funds with these red flags:
  - □ No long-term track record.
  - □ Front-end load or deferred sales charge, high 12b-1 fees.
  - □ A 15 percent loss in any single year.
  - □ Change in management or investment policies.
  - □ A 15 percent cumulative loss any time in the last 10 years.
  - □ Expense ratio of more than 1.5 percent for any fund over $30 million in assets.
  - □ High leverage (borrowing) to buy securities.
- □ Full speed ahead when you see these green lights glowing:
  - □ Ten-year performance that equals or exceeds market indexes.
  - □ Investment policy you understand and agree with.
  - □ Performance that beat indexes in the last bear market.
  - □ Stable management team.
  - □ Reasonable cost structure.
- □ Don't get caught up in the risk/reward myth. You don't have to gamble to get a good return. Most investors are wiser to stick with portfolios of conservative mutual funds.
- □ You have to pull the trigger. There comes a time when action is required. Have faith in your judgment. But when you send off your money, take precautions. It's your money, so play it safe.
- □ Once you've made an investment, watch it like a hawk. Each quarter, take 60 minutes off from watching television, and do your homework.

- Your motto should be, Do it right the first time. It doesn't take that much time to keep good records for performance tracking and tax record keeping. As soon as you invest, set up files for each fund.
- If you rely on brokers, it may cost you money. Don't fall for any high-pressure sales job. Remember, brokers are primarily salespeople, not objective advisers.
- No-load mutual funds have equal or better performance records, on average, than load funds.
- Plan for the future. It has a way of catching up to you. Save and invest now, or scrimp later. Use every opportunity available to put money in a tax-deferred retirement plan. If you have a company-sponsored retirement plan, be an activist. It's your money.
- Don't forget to rifle in on these investment essentials:
  - Develop a clear understanding of your objectives.
  - Establish a long-term strategy based on objective sources of information.
  - Execute your strategy with patience and emotional control.

Through good times and bad, panics and crashes, bull markets and bears, the most important factors in your success, both as a human being and as an investor, are desire, drive, and determination. If you have these three traits, you can build an investment portfolio that's like a sturdy, well-designed ship. It doesn't matter whether it's a sloop, schooner, sampan, or scow; whatever boat you're on should be able to ride out a brutal, stormy night with a minimum of damage, and sail swiftly when dawn brings a favorable tide.

Make this your goal, for yourself, for your family, and for your future. I know you can succeed.

Appendix A
How to Select
Mutual Funds Using
Mutual Fund Values

Mutual Fund Values (Don Phillips, Editor) is an excellent source of information on mutual funds (biweekly, $325 per year). It does for mutual funds what *Value Line* does for stocks. And this is one of the few sources for information on a mutual fund's portfolio manager and how long he or she has been running the fund. You can obtain more information by calling or writing:

> *Mutual Fund Values*
> 53 West Jackson Blvd.
> Chicago, IL 60604
> (312) 427-1985
> $325 per year (biweekly)

One page tells it all. Each of the over 1,000 mutual funds covered has its own one-page summary, which is updated periodically. The information is pulled together in a focused, visually stimulating format that shows past performance, a statement of investment objectives, *Mutual Fund Values* analysis of the fund, its largest portfolio holdings, the fund's address and telephone number, and much more statistical information.

The analysts at *Mutual Fund Values* give each fund a rating for risk and return. These are useful, but you should not rely on them slavishly. A number of great funds would have gotten average ratings from time to time based on the *Mutal Fund Values* system. Because they include many load mutual funds, you have to weed those out if you are looking just for no-load funds. Also, there could be a strong temptation to rely solely on their five-star ratings and not do your own research.

Before using *Mutual Fund Values*—whether you choose to subscribe or your public library carries it—you need to set your investment objectives as we discussed in Chapter 4. Once that is done, the folks at Morningstar (the publisher of *Mutual Fund Values*) recommend you start with their top-rated (five stars is tops) "all-weather" mutual funds. This is printed on page 3 of each issue's Summary Section. In this section, funds are divided into two groups—equity and hybrid funds and bond funds.

Here is an excerpt from them on how to use *Mutual Fund Values*.

We recommend that investors build their portfolio around a base of all-weather funds, such as those on our five-star list, which is printed on page 3 of each issue's Summary Section. By reading the individual page analyses of these funds, investors can identify those that suit their individual preferences. We recommend combining higher-rated mutual funds with contrasting styles to forge a solid base. For example, an investor might combine an all-weather small-cap fund, such as Acorn Fund, and a larger-cap fund like Partners with a diversified international fund like T. Rowe Price International Stock Fund and a turnaround-focused fund like Gabelli Asset Fund. Our fund reviews will help investors identify which funds bear which traits. In addition, we provide screens on pertinent investment criteria, such as P/E, price/book ratio, earnings growth, market capitalization, and return on assets, in each Summary Section.

After an investor has formed a solid base using our five-star funds, we recommend tailoring the portfolio with funds geared to meet more specific needs. For example, income-oriented investors can scan for higher-rated funds with high levels of income distributions. Aggressive investors can scan for funds with higher return potential, as seen in the earnings growth and return on assets records of their holdings. While funds that stress either growth or income may not be the best all-weather vehicles, they can be very valuable in finishing a diversified portfolio of mutual funds.

Once the portfolio is in place, monitoring is a relatively simple practice. Readers will want to track their own funds to keep abreast of changes in management or philosophical direction. It is also helpful to read our regular commentaries that point out trends in the industry or financial markets, as well as identifying funds of special interest. By assembling a sound portfolio to begin with, investors assure themselves of relatively easy maintenance.

Mutual Fund Values is a wonderful tool for researching great mutual funds. It is, however, rather expensive at $325 per year. Perhaps you could recommend your public library begin subscribing, or go in with a few friends. But if you are making substantial mutual fund investments, it could well be worth several times the price.

Appendix B
How to Select
Mutual Funds Using
The Handbook For No-Load Fund Investors

The Handbook for No-Load Fund Investors (Sheldon Jacobs, Editor) has been a superb resource for many years (annual, $38). In addition, they publish a monthly newsletter (12 issues, $62). You can obtain more information by calling or writing:

> *The Handbook for No-Load Fund Investors*
> P.O. Box 283
> Hastings-on-Hudson, N.Y. 10706
> (914) 693–7420

In the *Handbook*, they make an excellent case for using no-load mutual funds. And there are good explanations of the different fund categories. The Handbook has a good performance-ranking section by fund category. So you can go through and select the top 5 or 10 performers from a specific category, such as growth-income funds. There is also a handy section that lists pertinent information (address, telephone, investment objective, minimum-purchase requirement, expense ratio, portfolio manager and much more).

Here is an excerpt from the *Handbook* on how to select a portfolio of no-load mutual funds

Here are the steps necessary to initiate a no-load investment program. Each will be discussed in detail in subsequent chapters.

1. Analyze your specific investment objective. How much risk are you willing to take? Will you accept great risks for maximum gains, or would you prefer a more conservative course of investing with less risk and less potential?

2. Learn to recognize which mutual funds are designed to meet your specific investment objective. This is the most important step and the one most often neglected. Far too many investors have unknowingly bought funds either too speculative or too conservative for them, and their investment programs have suffered as a result.

3. Select no-load funds whose objectives coincide with your own. No matter what your investing style, allocate a major percentage of your assets into a *core holding* of mutual funds that you can hold long-term throughout both bull and bear markets. These are generally conservative funds, or sometimes more aggressive funds that do their own market timing, (that is, they sell stocks and sit with cash when market conditions are uncertain or adverse). In addition, asset allocation funds can be used as core holding.

4. Analyze past performance to determine the best two or three funds among those that meet your objective.

5. Learn the criteria for selecting those funds that are most likely to perform well in the future.

6. Write or phone for prospectuses of two or three top-performing funds.

7. Read the prospectus, in particular the sections detailing the fund's investment philosophy and allowable investments. Look carefully to see if the fund lists a 12b-1 fee and the percent of the fund's assets that have been drained for expenses—the expense ratio.

8. Then make a decision and invest in one or more funds.

9. Continue to follow the performance of these and other top-ranked funds in future issues of the *Handbook*.

With this plan of action you can design your own financially rewarding investment program.

The Handbook For No-Load Fund Investors is a very reasonably priced resource for mutual fund information. Also, its Section III provides a very detailed discussion of investing in no-load mutual funds. It is well worth the purchase price.

Glossary of Mutual Fund Terms

NAV/OFFERING PRICE When you look at mutual fund quotations in the paper, you will see two headings for share prices. For example, the *Wall Street Journal* uses NAV (net asset value) and Offer Price. Mutual funds with front-end loads will have two prices listed, with the higher one being the offer price, which includes the commission. No-load funds or funds with deferred contingent sales charges will have just one price listed.

AUTOMATIC REINVESTMENT One of the big advantages of mutual funds is the ability to reinvest dividends and capital gains distributions. Instead of being paid out to you, dividends are used by the fund to automatically buy more shares for you.

CAPITAL GAINS DISTRIBUTIONS When a mutual fund sells an investment for a profit, it realizes a capital gain for tax purposes. To avoid paying taxes on the gain, the fund must distribute virtually all of it to shareholders. Most mutual funds distribute these capital gains once a year.

CLOSED-END INVESTMENT COMPANY These are investment companies that issue a limited number of shares which are traded on an exchange or on the over-the-counter market. The company has no obligation to buy back shares. (See Open-End Investment Company.)

CUSTODIAN Mutual funds are obligated to provide for the physical protection of cash and securities. Most funds use a bank as custodian, although some of the larger mutual fund families have organized an affiliate that provides this function.

DIVERSIFICATION Known as the first rule of investing, diversification is a way of reducing the risk that any single stock or bond would drop precipitously and endanger the security of your portfolio. Most mutual funds are highly diversified and seldom have more than five percent of assets in any one stock or bond.

PERIODIC OR DOLLAR-COST AVERAGE INVESTING Many investors make a personal commitment to invest a given dollar amount each month or year, no matter what market conditions are. This approach, if applied with discipline, is excellent for building a solid portfolio. It does, however, require good record keeping.

EXCHANGE PRIVILEGE Mutual fund families generally allow shareholders to transfer from one fund in the family to another. There are usually restrictions on how often the privilege can be exercised.

INCOME DIVIDENDS When a mutual fund earns dividends or interest from investment, this is considered taxable income for tax purposes. To avoid paying taxes on the income, the fund must distribute virtually all of it to shareholders. Most mutual funds distribute income dividends quarterly.

INVESTMENT ADVISER Mutual funds hire investment advisers to make investment and asset-allocation decisions. Though the fund and its board of directors technically "hire" the investment adviser, in practice most mutual funds were founded by their investment advisers.

INVESTMENT OBJECTIVE Usually this is stated on the first or second page of the fund's prospectus. Typical objectives are high current income or long-term capital appreciation.

MANAGEMENT FEE This fee, on average about 0.5 percent of a mutual fund's assets, is paid to the fund's investment adviser.

NET ASSET VALUE PER SHARE (NAV) This is the market value of a mutual fund's total net assets, divided by the number of shares outstanding.

OPEN-END INVESTMENT COMPANY The technical or legal description of a mutual fund. The term open-end refers to the fact that this type of fund stands ready to buy back (at the NAV) as many shares as investors want to sell, at the same time also selling shares (at the NAV plus sales charge, if any) to all investors who want to buy in.

PROSPECTUS A legal document that discloses information the Securities and Exchange Commission believes any mutual fund should give to prospective investors. It covers investment objectives, shareholder services, investment restrictions, the names of officers and directors, fund expenses, management fees and other costs, financial statements, information on how to buy or redeem shares, and other information. In addition, mutual funds also must produce and distribute, upon request, a statement of additional information.

SALES CHARGE OR LOAD A commission paid to a member of a mutual fund's sales force, or to the fund itself or an affiliate. Some loads are a flat percentage, while others are a declining percentage depending on either the amount you invest or the length of time you remain in the fund.

TRANSFER AGENT. An organization, generally a bank, that is hired by a mutual fund to prepare and maintain shareholder account records.

12B-1 FEE A fee arising from a 1980 Securities and Exchange Commission ruling that permits mutual funds to pay certain expenses and distribution costs out of fund assets.

Index